JUSTICE OR TYRANNY?

Kennikat Press
National University Publications
Political Science Series

JUSTICE OR TYRANNY?

A CRITIQUE OF JOHN RAWLS'S
A Theory of Justice

DAVID LEWIS SCHAEFER

National University Publications
KENNIKAT PRESS // 1979
Port Washington, N. Y. // London

The author and publisher acknowledge, with thanks, the coopera-
tion of Belknap Press of Harvard University Press and Clarendon
Press, Oxford, in granting permission to quote extensively from *A
Theory of Justice* © 1971 by the President and Fellows of Harvard
College.

Manufactured in the United States of America

Published by
Kennikat Press Corp.
Port Washington, N. Y./London

Library of Congress Cataloging in Publication Data

Schaefer, David Lewis, 1943–
    Justice or tyranny?

    (National university publications)
    Bibliography: p.
    Includes index.
    1. Rawls, John, 1921– –a theory of justice.
2. Justice. I. Title.
JC578.R383S3   340.1'1   78-25903
ISBN 0-8046-9221-1

*This book is dedicated to
my mother and father,
who taught their children to love
both justice and wisdom.*

CONTENTS

PREFACE

This book is the culmination of a number of critical studies I have done over the years of John Rawls's writings about justice, beginning with a critique of Rawls's article "Constitutional Liberty and the Concept of Justice" that I submitted as an undergraduate honors thesis at Cornell University in 1964.[1] As the pages that follow will make evident, this attention to Rawls has not been motivated by the belief that his work is particularly profound. I have thought it worthwhile to study Rawls's writings closely, however, because they embody what I believe to be both a popular yet seriously deficient political ideology and a widely shared yet grossly inadequate understanding of the nature of political philosophy. In the process of trying to uncover the reasons underlying the deficiencies of Rawls's teaching, I have found that my understanding of the nature of political philosophy in its true form, as well as my comprehension of what is wrong with contemporary academic political thought, has deepened. I hope that others may gain some of these same benefits from reading this book.

I conceive of this book as a kind of apologia or defense of political philosophy. Political philosophy has few overt enemies nowadays. But this does not make its situation any less tenuous. Political philosophy needs to be defended today, not primarily against outward enemies, but against purported friends who misunderstand and consequently misrepresent its nature.

Philosophy—literally, the love or pursuit of wisdom—once was understood as a grand but exceedingly difficult and dangerous enterprise. Its grandeur and its difficulty were seen to stem from its perhaps Sisyphean quest to comprehend the whole of things in the light of reason. Its danger arose from the fact that in pursuing such understanding, the philosopher inevitably questions the beliefs that his fellow men hold most dear—especially their beliefs about the good, the just, and the holy. Hence the fate of Socrates was seen by his student Plato—the author of a far greater apologia than I could ever hope to produce—to be a permanent possibility for anyone who dared to emulate his way of life.

To someone living in one of the liberal regimes of the twentieth century, such dangers appear exceedingly remote. As heirs of the Enlightenment we inhabit societies founded on the belief that there is no tension, but rather a beautiful harmony, between philosophy and political society. Far from persecuting seekers after knowledge, our governments encourage and reward them with honors and fellowships. Far from scorning such individuals, the populace pays to have them educate their young in colleges and universities. While some technological byproducts of the pursuit of knowledge, such as the hydrogen bomb or LSD, are seen to be unfortunate, and the value of others, like television, is at best ambiguous, we remain committed to the principle that the well being of our societies depends on the continued progress of knowledge.

This revaluation of the pursuit of knowledge came about, however, only as the result of its transformation. Our present academic disciplines arose from a divorce, established at the outset of modernity, between philosophy and science. That form of the pursuit of knowledge that is most responsible for its revaluation is modern natural science, i.e., the pursuit of certain, but metaphysically neutral, knowledge of nature, with a view to mastering nature so as to promote what Francis Bacon called "the relief of man's estate."[2] The success of modern natural science in contributing to the conquest of nature has in turn inspired a reconstruction of the humanistic disciplines in an effort to make them similarly successful. The failure of the latter reconstruction to realize the hopes of its original proponents has hardly damped the enthusiasm of contemporary practitioners. But in the process the discipline known as philosophy has radically shrunk in scope and intent. Once equated with the pursuit of knowledge, philosophy is now essentially limited to what is left over after the various sciences have marked off their respective spheres. That remnant generally consists either on the one hand of sententious moralizing, the construction of utopias, and vague talk about values; or, on the other, of the quasi-scientific but purely formal analysis of words, concepts, and the epistemological assumptions of the other sciences.

If calling oneself a philosopher sufficed to make one so, it would seem at first as if the state of philosophy was never more prosperous than it is today. Whereas philosophers were once exceedingly rare, earned little or no living from their enterprise, and risked being persecuted for their occupation, they are now produced by the hundreds each year in the United States alone, aided by government financing. The major problem facing them, it would seem, is a surplus of prosperity: so legion is their number that they literally constitute a glut on the market.[3]

Unfortunately, the prosperity of philosophy has been purchased at the price of its truncation, not only as a discipline but also as a way of life. In order to appreciate this truncation, one would do well to study part 6 of Friedrich Nietzsche's *Beyond Good and Evil,* entitled "We Scholars." Nietzsche understood what has by now been almost forgotten: the radical difference between what it is to be and live like a philosopher, on the one hand, and merely to earn a Ph.D. in philosophy, on the other. Professors who casually refer to themselves as philosophers and write of Plato or Locke as if the latter were (at best) their equals, reveal a regrettable unawareness of the difference, and a consequently deficient measure of humility.

It is not only philosophy itself that has suffered from this truncation. Modern politics, unlike pre-modern politics, is essentially ideological in character. The dominant political ideas that move men nowadays are the popularized, watered-down, and often incoherently blended product of the teachings of various modern philosophers (such as Locke, Rousseau, Marx, and Nietzsche) who—unlike their classical and medieval predecessors—intended to transform the character of political life through the effects of their teachings. Whatever the particular merits of each of these profound men's teachings, an unfortunate effect of their very success in getting those teachings popularly accepted is that we have forgotten the philosophic roots, and hence the essential *questionableness,* of our contemporary dogmas.

The clearest evidence of this fact is the common misuse of the term "ideology" as a synonym for philosophy. Such usage implies either an unawareness or a denial of the difference between a rational account of the whole of things and a merely popular doctrine that either comforts people or else moves them to action. Those who employ it evince either an ignorance of the nature of philosophy, or else a presupposition that political philosophy as traditionally understood has been proved to be impossible.

If political philosophy is indeed impossible, then the human situation is much direr than those who presuppose its impossibility seem to realize. If it is impossible for man to achieve rational knowledge of his place in the whole of things, and of how he should live and be governed, then we cannot, in the fundamental sense, be free. We are doomed, in that case, to be the slaves of whatever political dogmas our historical epoch, our social environment. or our particular psychology compels us to accept.

For much of this century the impossibility of political philosophy was one of the express presuppositions of the dominant school of Anglo-American philosophy, the logical positivist movement. Insisting on the radical disjunction between facts and values, the adherents of this movement denied that rational knowledge of right and wrong, good and bad, was in any way accessible to man.

Recent years have witnessed a reaction against logical positivism in Anglo-American philosophy departments, stimulated by the later thought of Ludwig Wittgenstein. An increasing number of members of the so-called analytic school purport to "do" (as they put it) political philosophy. And, by most accounts, Rawls's *A Theory of Justice* constitutes the finest product of their work to date.

As the remainder of this book will make clear enough, I do not accept the proposition that either *A Theory of Justice* itself or the broader approach that it represents are truly deserving of the title of political philosophy. Rawls's approach, as I shall try to demonstrate, embodies the same fundamental dichotomy between facts and values that characterized the positivist school. But Rawls is unwilling to own up to this dichotomy. Rather than admitting that political beliefs cannot, by his criteria, be demonstrated to be objectively true or false, he traces his own beliefs to what he calls his "sense of justice," and treats the dictates of his idiosyncratic "intuition" as if they were equivalent to the truth about the good and the just. Philosophy as Rawls understands it is indeed, I shall contend, indistinguishable from ideology.

At the outset of my endeavor to articulate the nature of political philosophy by distinguishing it from a contemporary substitute, it is a pleasant duty to acknowledge my indebtedness to several great teachers who decisively shaped my own understanding of the "architectonic science." Whatever comprehension I possess of the writings of the great political philosophers and of the most serious American political thinkers is due in considerable measure to the teaching of Professors Joseph Cropsey and Allan Bloom, and of the late Professors Leo Strauss and Herbert Storing. Anyone who has known these men will know that whatever defects the present book may possess are attributable to the ignorance of the author rather than any failing on the part of his teachers. But it must also be said that I, along with many others who were fortunate enough to study under them, am heavily indebted to these men for teaching me what too few ever have the opportunity to learn: how to read and appreciate a serious book.

Having tried to indicate the extent of my debt to my teachers, I would like to express my gratitude to the sources of other kinds of support that made this book possible. The writing was assisted by a faculty fellowship, a summer research grant, and a research support grant awarded me by Holy Cross College. In addition, the research and previous articles on which the book is based were supported by summer research grants from the Earhart Foundation and Temple University. I am deeply appreciative of the assistance given me by each of these institutions. I would also like to thank Mrs. Jane Iannini for typing the manuscript, and Mrs. Selina Martin for her library assistance.

Support of a different kind, but for which I am also deeply grateful, was given me by my wife Roberta throughout this project. Her constant encouragement and her endeavor, amidst many difficulties, and at no small inconvenience to her own career, to provide an atmosphere conducive to the conduct of my work, contributed enormously to whatever merit this book may have. And my daughter Naomi also contributed to the completion of this book in a way that she will some day be old enough to understand.

JUSTICE OR TYRANNY?

ABOUT THE AUTHOR

David Lewis Schaefer is Associate Professor of Political Science at Holy Cross College, Worcester, Massachusetts. The recipient of a Ph.D. from the University of Chicago, he has published many articles on political philosophy in scholarly journals, and is the editor of *The New Egalitarianism: Questions and Challenges* (Kennikat Press, 1979). He has also been awarded research fellowships by the National Endowment for the Humanities and the Earhart Foundation.

INTRODUCTION

Americans do not think of themselves, and have not commonly been thought of by others, as a philosophic people. Early in our national history the French observer Alexis de Tocqueville commented as follows: "I think that there is no country in the civilized world where less attention is paid to philosophy than in the United States. The Americans have no philosophical school of their own, and they care little for all the schools that divide Europe, the names of which they hardly know."[1]

Since Tocqueville's time little would seem to have changed so as to invalidate his observation. The American people traditionally pride themselves on their pragmatism and Yankee ingenuity, showing a distrust for impractical theories and utopian ideologies. Some scholars, in fact, have attributed the very success of the American polity to its resistance to philosophic speculation about politics. In Louis Hartz's words, "Law has flourished on the corpse of philosophy in America."[2]

Every major American college and university, to be sure, now possesses a department of philosophy. But the analytic approach that dominates most American philosophy departments—an approach that originated in England earlier in this century—has always seemed rather modest in its claims, certainly very far from aspiring to philosophy's traditional role as queen of the sciences. And there is scant evidence that the academic study of philosophy in this country has exerted any influence on American political life—in contrast to the situation, say, in France.

In view of these facts, it is all the more surprising to observe the reception that has greeted a work entitled *A Theory of Justice,* written by a Harvard professor of philosophy named John Rawls and published in 1971. From the beginning Rawls's book received acclaim and attention unprecedented for a work of its sort. An endless succession of philosophy professors contributed (and continue to contribute) their interpretations and evaluations of the book to the professional journals of their discipline. More striking, in view of the usual isolation of academic fields from one another, is the amount of attention devoted to Rawls's work by scholars in other disciplines. Professional journals in a wide variety of these disciplines, including political science, law, sociology, economics, and public administration, have allocated enormous amounts of space to reviews, review-essays, symposia, and critical studies on *A Theory of Justice*. To cite a few representative examples: the *Yale Law Journal* and the *Quarterly Journal of Economics* each printed two lengthy review essays on the book; the *American Political Science Review*, seven.[3] And in a symposium on "Social Equity and Public Administration" in the *Public Administration Review*, *A Theory of Justice* was taken to provide the "most promising . . . ethical paradigm" for the reform of public organizations,[4] even though Rawls nowhere explicitly discusses the subject of public administration.

Even more surprising is the attention paid to Rawls's work in more popular media of opinion. As the editor of a book on Rawls has remarked:

However highly regarded by academics, scholarly works in moral and political philosophy, especially those emerging from the Anglo-American "analytic" tradition, *never* receive rave, lead reviews in the *New York Review of Books,* the *New York Times Book Review,* or *The Times Literary Supplement,* as *A Theory of Justice* did. Nor are they enthusiastically greeted by reviews in *The Economist,* the *Spectator, Nation, New Republic, Listener, New Statesman, Washington Post, Observer, The Times Higher Education Supplement,* and many others [as this book was].[5]

Typical of the reaction to *A Theory of Justice* in these media were the remarks of Marshall Cohen, who in his *New York Times* review called the book "magisterial," "peerless," and representative of Rawls's "notable contributions" to the "renewal of political philosophy."[6] Similarly, Stuart Hampshire, writing in the *New York Review of Books,* called *A Theory of Justice* "the most substantial and interesting contribution to moral philosophy since the war, at least if one thinks only of works written in English." In Rawls's work, according to Hampshire, "the substance of a critical and liberal political philosophy is here argued with an assurance and breadth of mind that put the book in the tradition of Adam Smith and Mill and Sidgwick."[7]

Neither the admiring reviewers just quoted nor most of Rawls's other critics gave the book unmixed praise. Indeed, *A Theory of Justice* spawned what has been termed an industry of criticism in which scholars competed to uncover defects in Rawls's argument. But curiously, practically none of these critics ever challenged the essential greatness and enormous value of the book. Most of Rawls's critics have exhibited a syndrome that is aptly described by Michael Zuckert:

Seldom has a book been more thoroughly refuted. Critics, of every philosophical persuasion, from nearly every contemporary political perspective, have found Rawls's premises and assumptions as safe a base for an argument as the San Andreas Fault for a nuclear power plant. They have found the structures built on those foundations about as solid as a Hollywood movie set. And yet, like Tertullian facing Christian dogma, or the average Californian, they believe.[8]

As striking examples of this syndrome, Zuckert cites two of Rawls's critics who represent sharply differing political perspectives. Brian Barry, whose book *The Liberal Theory of Justice* is dedicated to a critique of Rawls's position, finds "that Rawls's 'theory of justice' does not work and that many of his individual arguments are unsound." Nonetheless, he holds *A Theory of Justice* to be "a work of major importance," a "work of great significance for moral and political philosophy . . . worthy of [nothing] less than prolonged and intensive study," a work comparable to Hobbes's *Leviathan*.[9] Robert Nozick, writing from a "libertarian" point of view, is equally critical both of Rawls's overall theory and his particular arguments, yet finds the book to be "a powerful, deep, subtle, wide-ranging, systematic work in political and moral philosophy which has not seen its like since the writings of John Stuart Mill, if then. . . . Political philosophers must now work within Rawls's theory, or explain why not."[10] A third example to be added to those cited by Zuckert is Sidney Alexander, who calls *A Theory of Justice* a great work while undertaking to "challenge Rawls on almost every important point."[11]

As Zuckert suggests, the reception that *A Theory of Justice* has received stands in need of explanation. One is compelled to wonder why a 607-page work of abstract and often heavy-handed prose should elicit such widespread attention both from scholars outside Rawls's discipline and from the lay public. One is further curious as to why practically all of even those scholars who have criticized the deficiencies of Rawls's argument have seen fit to praise the work in terms like those employed by Barry and Nozick.

Surveying the Rawls literature, one finds two kinds of reasons given for attaching such value and importance to *A Theory of Justice*. In the first place, Rawls has been praised for supplying a theoretical, philosophical justification for the political beliefs that many well-intentioned men have previously held without such support. Hampshire, for instance, observes that "Professor Rawls arrives . . . at the principle of justice which social democrats have always groped for."[12] Second, Rawls's book has been hailed as marking the rejuvenation of political and moral philosophy as a substantive study in the English-speaking world, overcoming the indifference or irrelevance to political questions that had characterized philosophical works published earlier in this century that were influenced by the logical positivist movement. Hence *A Theory of Justice* demonstrates, according to Marshall Cohen, "how wrong it was to claim, as so many were claiming only a few years back, that systematic moral and political philosophy are dead."[13]

If Rawls has indeed succeeded in articulating a philosophic understanding of justice that can provide support for beneficent political action, then the praise his work has received is well earned. To anyone concerned about the eclipse of political philosophy in this century, which has left the title of political theorist to be taken over by "value-free" social scientists on the one hand and committed ideologues on the other, reports of the revival of Aristotle's architectonic science, if justified, will be further cause for rejoicing.

Unfortunately, I believe that the praise of *A Theory of Justice* on both these counts has been misguided. I do not believe that Rawls's account of justice is either coherent or salutary. More importantly, I think that Rawls's approach represents an utterly misleading understanding of the nature both of philosophy in general and of political philosophy in particular. The widespread acclaim that has greeted *A Theory of Justice* is not a measure of the book's real value, but attests rather to how widely political philosophy is misunderstood in the contemporary world.

Anyone who writes a book in order to attack another book—especially one so well received as *A Theory of Justice*—inevitably causes his own motives and intentions to be suspect. Such an enterprise, even if not impelled by sheer envy of another's success, is likely to seem like an attempt to reap a share in his rival's renown. After all, if Rawls's book is as bad as I claim it is, why should an author dedicate so much time, and so many pages, to demonstrating that fact—rather than simply ignoring it?

What makes a thorough critique of *A Theory of Justice* not only justifiable but essential, in my view, is the extent of its influence as well as the degree to which it reflects (as I have suggested) a widely shared misconception of the nature of philosophy.[14] My central concern is not to discredit Rawls, but to challenge his arguments and the view of philosophy on which they are based. The ultimate aim of this book is positive rather than negative: to contribute, to the extent that I can, to the recovery of political philosophy in its original and true character, by making clear how it differs from what goes by that title today. I hope to suggest, in the course of my argument, why such a recovery is most needful at the present time.

My critique of *A Theory of Justice* will proceed as follows: in chapter 1 I shall examine the way in which Rawls defines his purpose in *A Theory of Justice* and the underlying conception of political philosophy that the book embodies, concentrating particularly on the relation between moral theory as Rawls describes it and the sense of justice, the dictates of which such theory is intended to explicate. In this chapter I shall draw not only on parts 1 and 3 of *A Theory of Justice,* especially the section "Some Remarks about Moral Theory," but also on two earlier articles by Rawls that help to explain his approach. Chapter 2 will be devoted to the analysis of Rawls's purported derivation of the "principles of justice" from an "original position" in which men are said to be "fairly represented." This chapter is based largely on part 1 of *A Theory of Justice.* In chapter 3 I examine the practical political consequences that Rawls claims to infer from his previously established principles in part 2 of his book. I have also incorporated into this chapter my critique of the "difference principle" which Rawls originally stated in part 1, since his account and defense of that principle are largely independent of his description of the original position. Chapter 4 critically examines the conception of the good and the notion of moral education that Rawls sets forth most extensively in part 3. Finally, in chapter 5 I attempt to trace the particular defects I have noted both in Rawls's principles and in their consequences to what I believe is their underlying cause, the deficiency of Rawlsian moral theory as a substitute for political philosophy in the traditional sense.

The main body of my analysis is supplemented by two brief concluding sections. The epilogue sets forth some speculations about the roots of the contemporary political ideology that is largely responsible, I believe, for the acclaim that Rawls's book has received. In the appendix I examine Rawls's defense of his theory in a 1975 article entitled "Fairness to Goodness" and attempt to show that this article, while making clearer some of the problematic aspects of *A Theory of Justice,* refutes none of my criticisms of the book.

1

POLITICAL PHILOSOPHY
AND THE
SENSE OF JUSTICE

It is quite easy, upon accepted foundations, to build whatever one pleases.

Montaigne

As I have indicated in the introduction, the most surprising aspect of the reception that *A Theory of Justice* has received is the interest it seems to have provoked in the non-academic public. This interest is surprising not only in view of the traditional lack of interest in philosophy among Americans, but also on account of the peculiarly academic or technical character of Rawls's approach to philosophy. It is true that, as Norman Daniels observes, part of the reason for the "unusually wide interest shown in Rawls's work" is the perception that his book is *more* substantive, and hence less simply academic, than most recent Anglo-American work on philosophy.[1] Yet Daniels himself finds "irony in the perception that Rawls' work marks a major break with the recent trend of technical philosophy." since "the book is far more philosophically and technically sophisticated than it might seem to be at first reading." While striving to be "substantive," Rawls (Daniels remarks) "does not at all abandon the sophisticated apparatus and techniques of the professional philosopher...."[2]

Even a cursory look through *A Theory of Justice* will confirm Daniels's remarks about Rawls's reliance on a particular apparatus and set of techniques. Rawls employs a number of charts and graphs to illustrate his argument, and purports to draw heavily on information from the contemporary social sciences. And his approach to philosophy, according to Stuart Hampshire, falls "firmly within the traditions of analytic philosophy,"[3] a particular school of thought with its own characteristic methods and presuppositions.

What I have called the peculiarly academic character of *A Theory of Justice* is manifest most of all in the title of the book and Rawls's statement of his purpose in writing it. Both the title and the author's professed intention set *A Theory of Justice* markedly apart from most of the classic philosophic works of the Western tradition. Whereas Plato or Hobbes, for instance, spoke directly of what justice *is,* Rawls aspires rather to provide a theory of or about it. Furthermore, Rawls describes his guiding aim as being the provision of a superior alternative to prevailing theories of justice (3),[4] rather than the correction of some identifiable error in men's common opinions about what is just.

Neither Rawls himself nor the majority of his critics have displayed much awareness of the peculiarity of his approach, by comparison with the tradition of Western political philosophy. Rawls expressly compares his enterprise to that of such great modern political philosophers as Locke, Rousseau, and Kant (11), while asserting that his methodology conforms to that of Socrates and Aristotle (49, 51n.). A variety of other readers, both favorable and hostile, have similarly seen *A Theory of Justice* as falling squarely within one or another broad stream of the Western philosophic tradition.[5]

I believe that this failure to recognize what distinguishes Rawls's approach to justice from the older tradition stems from the almost universal acceptance by contemporary Anglo-American scholars in philosophy of the broad presuppositions of the analytic movement, presuppositions that are largely shared by Rawls. Daniels's description of Rawls's techniques as characteristic of the "professional" philosopher's approach in itself indicates how radically the understanding of philosophy has changed in recent times. Whereas philosophy was originally understood as a complete way of life, dedicated to the pursuit of truth about the whole of things, it is now a profession, a particular academic discipline among many, and a means of earning a living.[6] As a distinct academic specialty, philosophy inevitably has acquired its own "apparatus and techniques," which the unschooled layman can hardly hope to understand.

The widespread readership that *A Theory of Justice* has acquired outside the philosophic discipline seems to have been attracted not by the philosophical techniques by which Rawls derives his theory of justice, but by the substantive political discussion he professes to construct on the basis of that theory. As Daniels suggests, it is the "ideological import" of *A Theory of Justice,* as distinguished from its specifically philosophical content, that explains its appeal to the non-professional.[7] The popularity that the book has achieved seems to attest to the success with which Rawls has uncovered, as Daniels puts it, "the principles of justice which underlie the dominant moral and political views of our period."[8]

Philosophy, as distinguished from ideology, has traditionally been understood as an enterprise that aims to question men's dominant moral and political views, rather than presuming the truth of those views. Rawls himself seems to share this view of philosophy to some extent, since he proposes to inquire whether men's intuitive beliefs about justice are sound, thus leaving open the possibility that they will prove upon examination to be unsound (4). If we are to evaluate the validity of his account of justice, therefore, we are obliged to scrutinize the procedure by which he establishes his theory, rather than accepting this account merely because it seems to conform to the dominant views of our time. In order to achieve this goal we shall have to examine Rawls's methodology more closely than either most of his professional critics, who largely share his assumptions, or his non-professional ones, who seem uninterested in questions of philosophical technique, have generally done.

Since the beginning in such matters may be "more than half of the whole,"[9] it is necessary to pay particular attention at the outset to the manner in which Rawls has framed the fundamental problem that will concern him. That problem—the need for a more adequate theory of justice than has heretofore been available—is, I have suggested, a peculiarly academic one. This fact can be brought out most clearly by contrasting Rawls's problem with the questions that gave rise to political philosophy in its original form—classical political philosophy, as developed by Plato and Aristotle.

"Classical political philosophy," as Leo Strauss explains, "is characterized by the fact that it was related to political life directly. . . . The primary questions of classical political philosophy, and the terms in which it stated them, were not specifically philosophic or scientific; they were questions that are raised in assemblies, councils, clubs, and cabinets, and they were stated in terms intelligible and familiar, at least to all sane adults, from everyday experience and everyday usage."[10]

As an illustration of this point, one may note that the thematic discussion of justice in Plato's *Republic* arises initially out of the practical question of whether it is always just to give back what one has borrowed from other men. Similarly, the problem of justice in book 3 of Aristotle's *Politics* is seen to arise in connection with the conflicting claims of different classes to rule the city.[11] In each of these cases a philosophic inquiry into the nature of justice is shown to be necessitated by the unsatisfactory and contradictory character of common opinions about the debated issue.

Like his philosophic predecessors, Rawls refers at the outset to the practical importance of the subject of justice. "Justice," he observes, "is the first virtue of social institutions . . ."; he further asserts that "laws and institutions no matter how efficient and well-arranged must be reformed or abolished if they are unjust" (3). However, Rawls does not indicate any specific, substantive controversy, or any defect in what men think about justice, that necessitates a new philosophic inquiry into the subject. The sole practical problem to which he alludes by way of justification for his enterprise is the fact that "what is just and unjust is usually in dispute" in existing societies. Without alluding to any particular issue, Rawls asserts that disagreement about the meaning of justice prevents a society from being well ordered (5). The purpose of a theory of justice as Rawls understands it is therefore to promote a desirable social order by providing an account of justice on which all men can agree.

In this initial discussion Rawls does not attempt to explain the causes for men's failure thus far to agree on a conception of justice. In the concluding section of chapter 1 of *A Theory of Justice*, however, he seems to suggest that the failure is due to the defectiveness of the theories of justice that have thus far been developed. "Our present theories," Rawls asserts, "are primitive and have grave defects." He is particularly critical of the doctrine of utilitarianism, which he claims has "long dominated our philosophical tradition" despite its manifest defects, because no superior alternative theory has yet been propounded. In particular, among existing alternatives, "intuitionism is not constructive, perfectionism is unacceptable" (52).

I shall examine in the next chapter the particular meaning Rawls gives to each of these three leading theories. For the present, however, it suffices to note that none of the three is likely to be much more familiar in substance than it is in name to most people. Herein, therefore, lies one curiously academic feature of the way in which Rawls approaches the problem of justice. He seems to attribute the absence of agreement about justice within *society as a whole* to the defects of various theories that are known only to a particular circle of philosophical scholars. Yet this contention is on its face rather difficult to accept. Current disputes about justice in the United States, for instance, concern such issues as the severity of criminal sentencing, including the question of the death penalty; the justification of "benign" racial quotas in hiring and education; and the fairness of the tax laws. It is hard, on the surface, to see what connection any of these issues has with such theories as are mentioned by Rawls, or how a new theory could serve to resolve them.

Above and beyond this problem, Rawls's stated concern seems remote from everyday political life in another sense. It is doubtless the case that political life is rendered more difficult than would otherwise be the case by disputes about justice. Yet such disputes seem to be the very stuff of politics, and the notion of a society in which they could be eliminated sounds rather farfetched. More curious still is that what seems most to concern Rawls about such disputes is rather different from the concerns of most citizens who are actively involved in them. The primary goal of the direct participants in such disputes is normally that their own conception of what is just should be victorious. Less partisan participants in a debate about justice may be most concerned to determine what justice truly entails. The problem on which Rawls focuses attention as a justification for his inquiry, however—the need to secure men's *agreement* on a conception of justice—seems quite different from either of these goals.

These initial difficulties regarding Rawls's intention suggest the need to scrutinize more closely his conception of the nature and function of political or moral philosophy. Although it is ordinarily desirable, in analyzing a book, to try to conform as closely as possible to the order of presentation that the author himself has followed, the particular organization, or lack thereof, that characterizes *A Theory of Justice*[12] compels me to deviate from this procedure in order to try to clarify, at the outset, the character of the task that Rawls has set for himself. The fullest exposition Rawls provides of the nature of his enterprise is contained not at the beginning of the book, which seems to *presuppose* a particular understanding of philosophy, but in the concluding section of the first chapter, entitled "Some Remarks about Moral Theory." Moreover, Rawls's decision to avoid "extensive methodological discussions" in *A Theory of Justice* (p. ix) necessitates an examination of some of his other writings in order to elucidate that exposition.

Although Rawls once seems to describe his enterprise in *A Theory of Justice* as "substantive political philosophy" (202), he more commonly refers to it as moral theory. Regardless of this difference in terminology, however, moral theory as Rawls understands it seems to comprehend the subject matter traditionally assigned to political philosophy, since it entails not only an account of the meaning of justice, but also the description of how particular political institutions should be shaped to promote justice, properly understood. Despite the fact that Rawls distinguishes moral theory from moral philosophy in an article published subsequently to *A Theory of Justice*,[13] he seems in the book itself to equate the two, using the terms interchangeably (notably in "Some Remarks about Moral Theory"). Thus moral philosophy is given a provisional definition (to which Rawls seems to adhere throughout the book, although not in the subsequent article) as "the attempt to describe our moral capacity." Insofar as the moral philosopher is concerned with justice, therefore, "one may regard a theory of justice as describing our sense of justice"—i.e., one particular aspect of man's moral capacity (46). Considering its importance for his endeavor, Rawls provides surprisingly little information about the nature of this sense of justice. What explanation he provides in *A Theory of Justice* is contained in the following paragraph:

Let us assume that each person beyond a certain age and possessed of the requisite intellectual capacity develops a sense of justice under normal social circumstances. We acquire a skill in judging things to be just and unjust, and in supporting these judgments by reasons. Moreover, we ordinarily have some desire to act in accord with these pronouncements and expect a similar desire on the part of others. Clearly this moral capacity is extraordinarily complex. To see this it suffices to note the potentially infinite number and variety of judgments that we are prepared to make. The fact that we often do not know what to say, and sometimes find our minds unsettled, does not detract from the complexity of the capacity we have. [46]

Surely this discussion raises more problems than it settles. The phenomenon to which Rawls refers—a feeling that some things are just and others are not, and a sense of duty to act justly, or of guilt if we fail so to act—is familiar to all men. But if this sense is to serve as the foundation of Rawls's moral philosophy, one would expect him to examine it much more thoroughly. Is the sense of justice natural, or merely conventional? If the latter, then (as Glaucon suggests in Plato's *Republic*) would it not be the mark of a truly superior man to free himself from the constraints of justice in order to pursue his own interest?[14] This problem aside, to what extent can the sense of justice be relied on to provide *accurate* guidance regarding what is just? What degree of intellectual capacity is requisite to an effective sense of justice, and how many possess it?

Rawls answers the last of the questions above, after a fashion, simply by adopting an assumption later in the book: "I assume that the capacity for a sense of justice is possessed by the overwhelming majority of mankind . . ." (506). Evidently Rawls does not believe any great degree of intelligence is necessary for an effective sense of justice, but he provides no evidence to justify this assumption.

One might hope to find more satisfactory answers to the questions I have raised by turning to a lengthy section of the last part of *A Theory of Justice,* entitled "The Sense of Justice." Regrettably, however, little guidance regarding these problems is to be found there. In this section Rawls distinguishes between the answers given by two main traditions to the question of how men acquire moral sentiments: one which attributes the origin of these sentiments to societal expressions of praise and blame, and another which contends that they arise out of "the free development of our innate intellectual and emotional capacities according to their natural bent." Rather than trying "to assess the relative merits of these two conceptions of moral learning," Rawls finds it preferable "to try to combine them in a natural way." His own account of "the course of moral development," however, is entirely hypothetical: it is intended to show how such development *"might* occur in a well-ordered society" embodying Rawls's conception of justice, and "therefore *presupposes* the plausibility if not the correctness of this theory" (458-61; emphasis added). He proceeds to suggest how a person might acquire a sense of justice founded originally in the child's love for his parents and developed through his participation in a just "social arrangement." He further argues that to lack a sense of justice would mean "disfiguring ourselves" (489). But he explicitly abstains from deciding whether the sense of justice has any natural foundation (486). And he further observes that men's "present moral feelings are liable to be unreasonable and capricious" (490). The remainder of Rawls's discussion of the sense of justice is largely devoted to arguing that his own theory of justice would prove satisfying to men possessing such a sense, and hence that a society based on this theory would be stable.

The most important lack in the information Rawls supplies about the sense of justice concerns its epistemological status. Since Rawls himself alludes to the inevitability of conflict among different men's opinions about justice (355), it is difficult to understand how one might arrive at a satisfactory account of justice simply by describing a sense common to all men of a requisite age and intelligence. Nowhere in his thematic treatment of the sense of justice does Rawls provide evidence or argument to demonstrate that such a sense provides men with adequately objective guidance regarding what is just. In fact, his emphasis on the derivation of the sense of justice from one's upbringing and social environment would seem to suggest the opposite: would not the content of different men's sense of justice then be relative to the society in which they live, rather than being objective?[15]

Rawls's failure to answer these questions in *A Theory of Justice* compels us to look elsewhere for their illumination. As Rawls indicates in his preface, the argument of his book originally developed out of a series of articles he published during the two preceding decades (p. vii). Two of these articles, in particular, appear most relevant to our present inquiry.

One such article, entitled "The Sense of Justice," unfortunately adds little information to what is contained in the book. The starting point of this article, however, is somewhat suggestive. Rawls begins by citing Rousseau's view in *Émile* "that the sense of justice is no mere moral conception formed by the understanding alone, but a true sentiment of the heart enlightened by reason, the natural outcome of our primitive affections." Rawls endeavors in the first part of the article to "set out a psychological construction to illustrate the way in which Rousseau's thesis might be true."[16] This construction is similar to the account of moral development provided in *A Theory of Justice*.

These introductory remarks in "The Sense of Justice" are interesting primarily in a negative way. They indicate the degree to which Rawls lays stress on the emotive, as opposed to the "merely" rational, character of the sense of justice. And the article as a whole reveals a striking failure to consider how the emotive character of this sense might conflict with its rationality or objectivity.[17] *Émile* itself suggests that only by rigorously supervising a child's upbringing could one inculcate in him a sense of justice that would embody a proper appreciation of what is actually just. Contrary to Rawls's claim that men who pursue self-interest rather than justice would be "incapable of feeling resentment and indignation toward another's actions as being unjust,"[18] Rousseau indicates how, practically from the time of his birth, a human being possesses a potentiality for *unjust* indignation that only a carefully structured education could avert.[19] Thus we are still at a loss to understand Rawls's belief that the sense of justice possessed by men who have *not* necessarily had such an upbringing can provide an adequate foundation for a theory of justice.

Somewhat more helpful in elucidating the reasoning underlying Rawls's approach is an earlier article entitled "Outline of a Decision Procedure for Ethics." Rawls's stated purpose in this article is to discover "a reasonable method for validating and invalidating given or proposed moral rules and those decisions based on them" in order to resolve the much disputed issue of "the objectivity or the subjectivity of moral knowledge." The method he proposes is, first, to describe "a class of competent moral judges"; second, to define a "class of considered moral judgments" to be made by such judges by specifying the conditions in which these judgments are to be made; and third, "to discover and formulate a satisfactory explication of the total range of these judgments," an explication being defined as

a set of principles, such that, if any competent man were to apply them intelligently and constantly to the same cases under review, his judgments, made systematically nonintuitive by the explicit and conscious use of the principles, would be, nevertheless, identical, case by case, with the considered judgments of the group of competent judges [which latter judgments had been made intuitively].

Rawls expressly advocates in the "Decision Procedure" article that the degree of intelligence required to qualify a man as a "competent moral judge . . . should not be set too high, on the assumption that what we call 'moral insight' is the possession of the normally intelligent man as well as of the more brilliant." Presumably the "we" in this quotation are themselves men of normal intelligence using the term "moral insight" in some accustomed way. Yet Rawls provides no evidence to support his assertion, so as to show that most people would ordinarily regard Solomon (for instance) as no more of a competent moral judge than the average man-on-the-street.

An even more surprising feature of Rawls's notion of moral explication is his definition of the considered judgments that are to be explicated. Although a considered judgment must "be felt to be certain by the person making it," it must be "intuitive with respect to ethical principles, that is, . . . it should not be determined by a conscious application of principles so far as this may be evidenced by introspection." In other words, "a considered judgment does not provide any reasons for the decision. It simply states the felt preference in view of the facts of the case and the interests competing therein."

The reason Rawls defines considered judgments as not being based on a conscious application of a set of principles is to avoid the charge of circularity, since his aim is to derive the principles *from* such judgments. Yet there surely is something curious in a view that regards "considered" judgments as those which are based on feeling rather than reasoning. In fact, it seems difficult to reconcile this definition of a considered judgment with a condition for such judgments that Rawls lays down elsewhere in the same article: such judgments should concern "problems with which men are familiar and whereupon they have had an opportunity to reflect." If considered judgments involve reflection, then it would seem that the person making them should be able to state the reasons for his decisions as a result of his reflection. If not, then what would he reflect about?

By outlining a decision procedure for ethics, Rawls hoped in this article to discover an invariant element "in the considered judgments of competent [moral] judges," and therefore to demonstrate the existence of objective moral principles. At the time he did not claim to have proved the existence of such principles, but observed that "the belief that such an explication [of the invariant moral standard] does exist is perhaps a prerequisite for the finding of it, should it exist, for the reason that one who does not so believe is not likely to exert the great effort which is surely required to find it." As to those skeptics who point to the variation among moral codes and customs over time as evidence against such a belief, Rawls replied somewhat ambiguously: "...yet when we think of a successful explication as representing the invariant in the considered judgments of competent judges, then the variation of codes and customs is not decisive against the existence of such an explication."

The account of the methods and purposes of ethics in the "Decision Procedure" article provides, as Rawls acknowledges, the general point of view followed in his account of moral theory in *A Theory of Justice* (46n). As we have seen, Rawls regards the task of moral theory as being the description of the sense of justice that he assumes the vast majority of men possess. In *A Theory of Justice* he adheres to the view formulated in "Decision Procedure" that the way to arrive at such a description is to formulate a set of principles that conform to the considered moral judgments that men make. Here he defines such judgments as those "in which our moral capacities are most likely to be displayed without distortion" (47). The criteria for determining such judgments are primarily negative ones:

For example, we can discard those judgments made with hesitation, or in which we have little confidence. Similarly, those given when we are upset or frightened, or when we stand to gain one way or the other can be left aside. All these judgments are likely to be erroneous or to be influenced by an excessive attention to our own interests. Considered judgments are simply those rendered under conditions favorable to the exercise of the sense of justice, and therefore in circumstances where the more common excuses and explanations for making a mistake do not obtain. The person making the judgment is presumed, then, to have the ability, the opportunity, and the desire to reach a correct decision (or at least, not the desire not to). [47–8]

Each of these conditions conforms to principles laid down previously in "Decision Procedure." Interestingly, however, Rawls leaves out the condition laid down in "Decision Procedure" that considered judgments should simply state a felt preference without providing any reason for the decision. This omission seems to suggest a heightened view on Rawls's part of the importance of deliberation and reasoning in arriving at a correct moral judgment. That impression is strengthened by Rawls's elaboration of the relation between the moral principles the philosopher aims to construct and the judgments they describe. Those principles, he now holds, should match our considered judgments in a state of "reflective equilibrium" (20).

Rawls adopts the concept of reflective equilibrium out of recognition of what he calls the Socratic character of moral philosophy. "In describing our sense of justice," he observes, "an allowance must be made for the likelihood that considered judgments are no doubt subject to certain irregularities and distortions despite the fact that they are rendered under favorable circumstances." The judgments studied by the moral theorist do not have the fixed character of the phenomena investigated by the physical scientist (48–49). Rather, the formulation of a moral theory may itself produce some change in the judgments it is intended to describe:

When a person is presented with an intuitively appealing account of his sense of justice (one, say, which embodies various reasonable and natural presumptions), he may well revise his judgments to conform to its principles even though the theory does not fit his existing judgments exactly. He is especially likely to do this if he can find an explanation for the deviations which undermine his confidence in his original judgments and if the conception presented yields a judgment which he finds he can now accept. [48]

By terming moral philosophy a Socratic discipline, Rawls evidently means that it is dialectical in character: that is, the truth can be arrived at only through a continuous process of comparing and weighing disparate judgments with one another, and with the theory that is intended to describe them. A question remains, however, as to how far Rawls's and Socrates' understandings of philosophy are the same, as regards both its goal and its procedure. I shall consider this question at some length in chapter 5. At present it suffices to take note of what seem to be several manifest differences between Rawls's procedure and Socrates'. One such difference is that the acceptability of a theory of justice seems to depend, for Rawls, on whether it is intuitively appealing, rather than on whether it has been demonstrated by reason to be true. Furthermore, although Socrates indeed develops his account of justice in Plato's *Republic* by considering the opinions of his interlocutors, he nowhere represents this account as a description of their sense of justice. Finally, Rawls's description of men's moral *judgments* as the object of philosophic study, analogous to the physical phenomena studied by the natural scientist, seems to deny the existence of an objective *eidos* or essence of justice separable from men's judgments about it, such as Socrates endeavored to discover.

I believe that each of these differences creates serious difficulties with regard to the *rationality* of moral theory as Rawls understands it. As I shall try to demonstrate further on in this book, Rawls's peculiarly academic conception of political philosophy prevents him from adequately considering the diversity of men's substantive opinions about justice, and consequently from arriving at an objectively defensible account of justice. But these theoretical defects of Rawls's system can best be discussed in the light of an examination both of the procedure by which he constructs his theory of justice and of the substance of that theory. Hence I shall now turn to an analysis of these themes.

2

THE ORIGINAL POSITION
VERSUS THE STATE OF NATURE

Whatsoever therefore is consequent to a time of war, where every man is enemy to every man; the same is consequent to the time, wherein men live without other security, than what their own strength, and their own invention shall furnish them withal. In such condition, there is no place for industry; because the fruit thereof is uncertain: and consequently no culture of the earth; no navigation, nor use of the commodities that may be imported by sea; no commodious building; no instruments of moving, and removing, such things as require much force; no knowledge of the face of the earth; no account of time; no arts; no letters; no society; and which is worst of all, continual fear, and danger of violent death; and the life of man, solitary, poor, nasty, brutish, and short.

Hobbes, *Leviathan*

1

As we have seen, Rawls's stated purpose in *A Theory of Justice* is to devise a moral theory that will conform better to men's considered judgments of justice than existing theories do. The chief existing theories he considers, each of which he believes to be primitive and to possess grave defects, are utilitarianism, perfectionism, and intuitionism (52).

Although Rawls levels criticisms against each of these three theories, his particular concern is with one of them, utilitarianism, which "has long dominated our philosophical tradition. . . . despite the persistent misgivings that [it] arouses" (52). As we shall see, Rawls devotes much more attention to analyzing the defects of utilitarianism than to those of the other two theories. And he describes his particular aim as being the construction of "an alternative to utilitarian thought" in all its varieties (22).

Rawls identifies the essence of the classical utilitarian doctrine, which he finds most clearly stated by the nineteenth-century English theorist Henry Sidgwick, as the principle "that society is rightly ordered, and therefore just, when its major institutions are arranged so as to achieve the greatest net balance of satisfaction summed over all the individuals belonging to it" (22). "Utilitarianism" as Rawls understands it has a more specific and technical meaning than it does in ordinary parlance, as reflected, for example, in the *Oxford English Dictionary*'s definition of a utilitarian as "one who considers utility the standard of whatever is good for man; *loosely,* a person devoted to mere utility or material interests" (emphasis in original).

Rawls's attitude towards utilitarianism in this more general sense is not entirely clear. But his opinion of what he calls classical utilitarianism is sharply critical, on the ground that it contradicts men's deepest convictions about the primacy of justice. The essential problem in utilitarianism is that it is a teleological theory, i.e., one which defines "the right . . . as that which maximizes the good" (24–25). Interpreting the good as the greatest happiness of the greatest number of people, the utilitarian consequently understands as right or just whatever will promote that goal to the greatest extent. Utilitarianism as Rawls understands it views society as an organic whole in which the good of each particular member is to be evaluated purely in terms of its contribution to the greatest sum of utility for the community. "The striking feature of the utilitarian view of justice," Rawls finds, "is that it does not matter, except indirectly, how [the] sum of satisfactions is distributed among individuals . . ." (26). Consequently, while the utilitarian *may* adhere to "the protection of [the] liberties and rights" of all individuals as conducive to the greatest happiness of the whole, "there is no reason in principle why the greater gains of some should not compensate [according to the utilitarian formula] for the lesser losses of others; or more importantly, why the violation of the liberty of a few might not be made right by the greater good shared by many" (26).

The crux of Rawls's objection to utilitarianism is that it "does not take seriously the distinction between persons" (27). Utilitarianism fails to do justice to the "common sense" conviction that every individual possesses "an inviolability founded on justice or, as some say, on natural right, which even the welfare of every one else cannot override" (28). Even though Rawls can find no adherent of utilitarianism who advocated slavery, for instance, on the ground that the sacrifice of the slaves' well being would be more than made up for by the happiness which their enslavement brought to the master class, the classical utilitarian doctrine nonetheless leaves open the *possibility* that such an argument might be made. More generally, "the principle of utility asks" that some men "accept the greater advantages of others as a sufficient reason for [accepting] lower expectations over the course of [their] whole life. This is surely an extreme demand," one that Rawls believes conflicts with each man's sense of justice (178). It is chiefly in order to avert such possibilities that Rawls wishes to supplant the utilitarian doctrine with a new moral theory that will give adequate account to the primacy of justice, understood as the protection of the equal rights of all individuals, over the social good.

The root difficulty of utilitarianism—its teleological character—is one that Rawls finds common to another moral theory which he labels perfectionism. According to this doctrine, which Rawls attributes to such thinkers as Aristotle and Nietzsche, society is to be arranged "so as to maximize the achievement of human excellence in art, science, and culture" (25, 325). Here again, the problem is that the social good—now understood as human excellence rather than utility—might be used as a justification for denying to individuals the equal rights to which our sense of justice tells us they are entitled. Hence "to find a firm basis for equal liberty, it seems that we must reject the traditional teleological principles both perfectionist and utilitarian" (330).

Rawls understands teleological moral theories in contradistinction to what he calls "deontological" ones. "By definition . . . a deontological theory [is] one that either does not specify the good independently from the right, or does not interpret the right as maximizing the good" (30). By this rather awkward definition, Rawls evidently means that a deontological theory holds that justice or rightness is either an essential element of goodness or something independent of, and transcendent over, the good. According to such a theory, it could never be right to sacrifice the just deserts of individuals for the sake of promoting the social good.

The third particular sort of moral theory that Rawls considers, intuitionism, may be either teleological or deontological. Rawls's definition of this doctrine differs considerably from the one conventionally employed by most philosophical scholars.[1] Such epistemological doctrines as "that the concepts of the right and the good are unanalyzable," and consequently can be known only through intuition rather than reasoning, "are not," Rawls explains, "a necessary part of intuitionism as I understand it" (34–35). Rather, he treats intuitionism

as the doctrine that there is an irreducible family of first principles which have to be weighed against one another by asking ourselves which balance, in our considered judgment, is the most just. Once we reach a certain level of generality, the intuitionist maintains that there exist no higher-order constructive criteria for determining the proper emphasis for the competing principles of justice. . . . Intuitionist theories, then, have two features: first, they consist of a plurality of first principles which may conflict to give contrary directives in particular types of cases; and second, they include no explicit method, no priority rules, for weighing these principles against one another: we are simply to strike a balance, by what seems to us most nearly right. [34]

Rawls does not reject the intuitionist view out of hand. He urges, however, that "we should do what we can to reduce the direct appeal to our considered judgments" on which the intuitionist relies, lest it prove to be impossible to secure men's agreement to a common conception of justice:

For if men balance final principles differently, as presumably they often do, then their conceptions of justice are different. . . . If we cannot explain how [the] weights [to be assigned to different principles] are to be determined by reasonable ethical criteria, the means of rational discussion have come to an end. . . . We should do what we can to formulate explicit principles for the priority problem [of weighing principles against one another], even though the dependence on intuition cannot be eliminated entirely. [41]

Rawls believes he has devised a theory of justice that overcomes at the same time the defects both of intuitionism on the one hand and of utilitarianism and perfectionism on the other. This theory—first enunciated by Rawls, in a somewhat different form, in an article published in 1958— is what he calls "justice as fairness."[2]

The formula of justice as fairness would seem at first to be neither original nor controversial, since the two terms are often understood as being nearly synonymous with one another. What Rawls means by this formula, however, is something more particular. The true principles of justice, Rawls contends, are those that persons *"fairly situated* with respect to one another can agree to if they can agree to anything at all" (244; emphasis added). As he contended in the "Decision Procedure" article that I discussed in chapter 1, Rawls believes that reliable moral judgments are likely to be made only by persons who are in situations that render their reflections dispassionate and impartial. What he argues in *A Theory of Justice* is, in effect, that conditions analogous to those necessary to produce objective moral judgments in particular cases are necessary in order to elucidate objective *principles* of justice. To say that the conditions are analogous is by no means to say that they are the same: for instance, those who choose the principles of justice, unlike just judges in particular cases, must be "concerned to further their own interests" through their decision. But as we shall see, Rawls's notion of a fair decision-making situation is intended to prevent those who choose the principles of justice from advancing any *particular* interests at the expense of others. Thus there is a considerable parallel to the criteria for just decision making outlined in "Decision Procedure."

Rawls describes the aim of his theory as being "to present a conception of justice which generalizes and carries to a higher level of abstraction the familiar theory of the social contract as found, say, in Locke, Rousseau, and Kant." The contract he intends to formulate is not, however, "one to enter a particular society or to set up a particular government." Rather, the contracting parties are to agree on "the principles of justice for the basic structure of society," prior to any more specific decisions about particular political and social institutions (11).

By deriving the principles of justice from the hypothetical collective decision of persons fairly situated with one another, Rawls has endeavored to subsume moral theory under what he calls "the theory of rational choice" (16). The problem of justice, which has perplexed philosophers and divided political communities since the beginning of human time, now lends itself to resolution, Rawls believes, thanks to the development of one of the latest techniques of social science: game theory. (Herein lies another apparent reason for his identifying justness with fairness: Rawls compares the rules of justice to those of a "fair game" [304].)

Rawls's claim to have resolved the problem of justice through the application of game theory has understandably constituted one of the prime sources of the appeal of *A Theory of Justice* to social scientists, as well as being cited as evidence of the progress that philosophy has made thanks to its adoption of what Norman Daniels calls a "sophisticated apparatus and techniques." Even though contemporary social science may in itself be neutral with respect to questions of value, Rawls seems to have demonstrated that the *techniques* of social science (including economics, psychology, and "political sociology," as we shall see, as well as game theory) can be used to resolve the most fundamental moral and political dilemmas.

In the remainder of this chapter I shall scrutinize the procedure by which Rawls purports to derive the principles of justice from a social contract with the aid of game theory. By contrasting Rawls's procedure with the reasoning of the great social contract philosophers whom he purports to be improving upon, I shall endeavor to demonstrate that Rawls's claim to articulate the nature of justice in this manner is specious, and that the understanding of justice requires precisely the confrontation of the fundamental issues that Rawls endeavors by his technique to avoid. In so doing, I hope to suggest reasons for doubting that game theory in *any* form can be of much use in resolving the fundamental problems of political philosophy, or that the reliance on such techniques will be the means by which philosophy can progress.

2

The characteristic that most obviously distinguishes Rawls's account of a social contract from the account offered by the renowned modern philosophers to whom he alludes is that it does not rest on any examination of what an *actual* non-political condition or "state of nature" among men would be like. Rawls's procedure in this regard is in fact the opposite of that followed by his predecessors: instead of inferring the principles of the contract from what men, given their nature, would be likely to agree upon in the absence of an already existing government and set of laws, he freely constructs the character of the parties to a "purely hypothetical" "original position of equality" in order "to lead to a certain conception of justice" (12). That conception is to consist of

principles which . . . match our considered convictions of justice or extend them in an acceptable way . . . [so that] applying these principles would lead us to make the same judgments about the basic structure of society which we now make intuitively and in which we have the greatest confidence; or . . . in cases where our present judgments are in doubt . . . [would] offer a resolution which we can affirm on reflection. [19]

In other words, Rawls assumes from the outset (as I have noted in chapter 1) the rightness of the considered judgments that "we" confidently make and that stem from a sense of justice that is common to men generally. The aim of his account of the social contract will not be fundamentally to alter, but rather to systematize, those judgments by revealing the principles according to which men's sense of justice appears to operate [ix, 45–46].

The fact that the principles of justice need not be derived from any situation that is thought to be given by nature means that Rawls is free to alter any of the circumstances of the original position in which principles are to be chosen, should he not be satisfied with the principles to which a particular situation gives rise. He explains the complex interrelation between the original position or "initial situation" in which the principles of justice are to be decided on, and the considered judgments they are intended to explicate, as follows:

> In searching for the most favored description of this situation we work from both ends. We begin by describing it so that it represents generally shared and preferably weak conditions. We then see if those conditions are strong enough to yield a significant set of principles. If not, we look for further premises equally reasonable. But if so, and these principles match our considered convictions of justice, then so far well and good. But presumably there will be discrepancies. In this case we have a choice. We can either modify the account of the initial situation or we can revise our existing judgments, for even the judgments we take provisionally as fixed points are liable to revision. By going back and forth, sometimes altering the conditions of the contractual circumstances, at others withdrawing our judgments and conforming them to principle, I assume that eventually we shall find a description of the initial situation that both expresses reasonable conditions and yields principles which match our considered judgments duly pruned and adjusted. This state of affairs I refer to as reflective equilibrium. [20]

The relation between the initial situation and men's existing judgments of justice is evidently a circular one. On the one hand, since the original position is intended to produce principles of justice that largely conform to men's existing judgments, that position must be shaped by a cognizance of those judgments. On the other hand, since the value of a theory of justice lies in its ability to systematize men's judgments, it is hoped that those judgments will in part be altered, thanks to Rawls's account of the decisions made in the original position, to conform to the principles derived therefrom.

Given the purely heuristic purpose it is intended to serve, there is no reason, Rawls believes, why the original position should resemble any actual situation in which human beings might find themselves. Rawls in fact expressly warns against confusing "the motivation of the persons in the original position . . . with the motivation of persons in everyday life" (148). The original position "is not intended to explain human conduct except insofar as it tries to account for our moral judgments and helps to explain our having a sense of justice" (120). Consequently, the major problem Rawls faces in constructing the original position is not to analyze the way that human beings behave, but to shape this situation so that it will give rise to principles that conform to men's sense of justice.

In order to insure the establishment of principles of justice that are morally acceptable, Rawls omits from the circumstances of the original position all human desires, concerns, and characteristics that he believes are irrelevant "from a moral point of view" (120; 18-19). Because justice means fairness, and the essence of fairness (for Rawls) is equality, it is most important to rule out significant inequalities of ability from the circumstances of the original position. Hence he assumes that the parties to the original position are roughly similar in physical and mental powers, so that no one among them can dominate the rest. Rawls furthermore supposes that each of the parties is vulnerable to attack and to "having [his] plans blocked by the united force of others," and that they exist in a state of moderate scarcity of natural resources so that schemes of co-operation are feasible and mutually advantageous, and yet cannot fully satisfy "the demands men put forward" (127).

More curious than the preceding "objective circumstances" of the original position are the "subjective" circumstances that Rawls additionally assumes in order to insure the choice of principles of justice that will be independent of, and hence prior to, any particular understanding of the good. On the one hand, the parties have needs and interests that are either "similar . . . or . . . complementary, so that mutually advantageous cooperation among them is possible." On the other hand, these parties also possess "their own plans of life," or "conceptions of the good," which "lead them to have different ends and purposes, and to make conflicting claims on the natural and social resources available." In order to emphasize that each "self . . . regards its conception of the good as worthy of recognition" and its "claims . . . as deserving satisfaction," Rawls assumes "that the parties take no interest in one another's interests." Furthermore, their biases and the defects of their knowledge give rise to "a diversity of philosophical and religious belief and of political and social doctrines" (127). Rawls claims to make "no restrictive assumptions about the parties' conception of the good except that they are rational long-term plans," meaning that they are plans designed by each person to satisfy the greatest number of his desires (129, 143). These conceptions of the good may be egoistic or not, and can be as "irreconcilably opposed" as "the spiritual ideals of saints and heroes" (129). Rawls does assume, however, that being rational, the parties do not suffer from envy, since another person's well being does not affect one's own satisfaction of his desires (143). At the same time it is supposed that each person in the original position does care about the well being of some of those in the next generation after his own (128).

Rawls's account of the subjective circumstances of the parties in the original position stands greatly in need of clarification. Any attempt at such clarification would force Rawls to recognize that several of his assumptions are incompatible with one another. It is hard to see how much complementarity of needs or interests, or mutually advantageous cooperation, can exist among men whose aims might be irreconcilably opposed, or whose disagreement over religious and political and social doctrines is unlimited. It is difficult to understand how a saint or hero could take no interest in other men's well being, or that a man whose final purposes were "wealth, position, and influence, and the accolades of social prestige" (129) could be immune to envy, since the goods he aims at are essentially relative ones. Nor is Rawls's notion of rationality at all clear: why is it rational to aim to satisfy a greater number of one's desires, rather than regarding one aim as more important than all others?[3] Indeed, if rationality is purely an instrumental term (14), why is it rational to be "rational"?—in other words, why should one not have it as one's purpose to choose ineffective means to one's ends? Such a proposal makes no more but no less sense than does Rawls's doctrine, according to which (as he later indicates) it is perfectly rational to avoid deliberating or having a plan at all (418), or to spend one's life counting blades of grass (432) if one desires. Rawls grants that the latter enterprise, although rational, may be "peculiarly neurotic" (432). This is a strange kind of rationality, indeed.[4]

Greater difficulties emerge from a further condition that Rawls attaches to the original position which he calls the "veil of ignorance." In order to "nullify the effects of specific contingencies which put men at odds and tempt them to exploit social and natural circumstances to their own advantage" in an unjust way, Rawls assumes that no one in the original position "knows his place in society, his class position or social status, . . . his fortune in the distribution of natural assets and abilities, his intelligence and strength, and the like." Nor is he aware of "his conception of the good, the particulars of his rational plan of life, or even the special features of his psychology." This individual ignorance is supplemented by a collective ignorance to insure an impartiality among societies and generations in the choice of principles: "The parties do not know the particular circumstances of their own society . . . its economic or political situation, or [its] level of civilization and culture," nor do they have any "information as to which generation they belong [to] ." In fact, "the only particular fact which the parties know is that their society is subject to the circumstances of justice and whatever this implies" (137). Yet this artificial constriction of ignorance does not prevent the parties from possessing the most extensive kind of "general" knowledge, the only knowledge that Rawls believes is necessary for the proper choice of principles:

It is taken for granted . . . that they know the general facts about human society. They understand political affairs and the principles of economic theory; they know the basis of social organization and the laws of human psychology. Indeed, the parties are presumed to know *whatever general facts affect the choice of the principles of justice.* There are no limitations on general information, that is, on general laws and theories, since conceptions of justice must be adjusted to the characteristics of the systems of social cooperation which they are to regulate, and there is no reason to rule out these facts. [137–38; emphasis added]

Rawls anticipates the objection "that the exclusion of nearly all particular information makes it difficult to grasp what is meant by the original position" (138). To this argument he replies that "one . . . can at any time enter this position or . . . simulate the deliberations of this hypothetical situation, simply by reasoning in accordance with the appropriate restrictions" (138). But is it at all possible to reason in this manner? Can human beings possess any general knowledge without having derived or at least developed this knowledge from the study of particulars (a study in which the participants in the original position are prevented from engaging)? One cannot, for instance, have learned any laws of human psychology while remaining entirely ignorant of one's own psychology. But how, having derived one's knowledge from the awareness of particulars, can one forget the latter in order to simulate the deliberations of the original position? One might pretend or deceive oneself into believing that he had forgotten his particular beliefs and characteristics, but this pretense would not have the radically neutralizing effects Rawls desires. Furthermore, even if one could engage in this kind of temporary, partial memory lapse, it is doubtful that one would have any meaningful general knowledge left with which to deliberate. It is not at all evident that there are significant universal laws determining human behavior, individual or collective, with the same regularity that the laws of physics govern purely material things.[5] Thus it does not appear possible to devise even the most general principles for the regulation of a particular society, knowing nothing of that society's distinguishing characteristics.[6] It is even doubtful that general and particular knowledge are at all separable in the manner Rawls assumes, so that *any* knowledge would remain once the particulars had been subtracted. How, without a knowledge of particulars, would one even know to what things one's general knowledge referred? These are questions fundamental to the project of *A Theory of Justice,* but Rawls passes over the problems with little evidence of having reflected on them.

Besides the difficulties inherent in the notion of the veil of ignorance, it is incompatible with the other assumptions Rawls makes about the parties to the original position. Rawls has asserted that those parties have conceptions of the good that lead them to pursue different ends and purposes. He now adds that "the parties do not know their conception of the good," even though each party has one. But what can it mean to know that one has a conception of the good without knowing what that conception is? How could one even explain to someone who lacked any conscious conception of the good what a conception of the good is? Such difficulties with the central notion of Rawls's original position show it to be an inadequate basis for any sort of deliberation, simulated or otherwise.

In spite of all the problems above, Rawls thinks that "the veil of ignorance is so natural a condition that something like it must have occurred to many" (137n.). But nothing like it is to be found in the writings of Hobbes, Locke, Rousseau, or Kant. These philosophers did not need to resort to such a condition in order to demonstrate that it would be in the interests of all men, under the respective circumstances that each philosopher attempted to show were those of nature, to agree to a contract such as he described. By requiring men to choose a conception of justice without their being able to reflect on what things are substantively good for them as individuals, on the other hand, Rawls is demanding an impossibility. Consequently, as I shall attempt to demonstrate in the next section of this chapter, Rawls himself is compelled to violate his description of the original position in order to derive anything from it.

3

In determining the principles of justice that are to be chosen, Rawls conceives of the parties to the original position as if they were potential participants in a game, who are drawing up rules for the game without knowing what their particular roles in the game will be. Each participant is assumed to aim at maximizing his gains in the game of justice. Because "envy tends to make everyone worse off," Rawls has chosen to suppose that the parties are free from this passion: they "strive [only] for as high an absolute score as possible" without regard to the scores of their opponents (144). They are presumed, moreover, "to be capable of a sense of justice," so that they "can rely on each other to understand and to act in accordance with whatever principles are finally agreed to. . . . Their capacity for a sense of justice insures that the principles chosen will be respected" (145).

In order to estimate their potential gains under alternative sets of rules, the parties must have an index of points by which to keep score. Since the game of justice involves the distribution of good things, it would seem that they must know what things contribute to a good or happy life, and the relative importance of these various goods. Such knowledge has been ruled out, however, by the condition that the parties have different conceptions of the good and yet do not know what their respective conceptions are. Rawls attempts to resolve this difficulty by constructing an "index of primary goods" of which, he assumes, any rational person would want more rather than less for the attainment of his particular notion of the good, whatever it may be (155). These primary goods consist of "rights and liberties, powers and opportunities, income and wealth," and "self-respect" (92–93, 396).

In an effort to make the primary goods impartial among different particular conceptions of the good, Rawls has left this list so abstract as to be unhelpful as a basis for any kind of choice. In order to decide rationally on how to allocate such goods, one wants to know: a right to do what? A power or opportunity for what? But Rawls provides no answers. Nor, given the contentless character of Rawls's notion of rationality, is it evident how he can infer the desirability of a greater sum of primary goods from the concept of rationality (might one not, with perfect "rationality" and even simple reasonableness, believe that opportunities for material gain, including one's own, should be limited for the sake of improving the moral character of the citizenry?). Nonetheless, Rawls contends that, given the index of primary goods upon which to base their choices, the parties to the original position would be led by a rational view of their respective self-interests to agree on the two principles of justice that he lays out. The first of these principles[7] specifies that "each person is to have an equal right to the most extensive total system of equal basic liberties compatible with a similar system of liberty for all." The "priority" of this principle means that "liberty can be restricted only for the sake of liberty," and not for the sake of any other good. The second principle, relating to the distribution of primary goods other than liberty, consists of two parts: "Social and economic inequalities are to be arranged . . . to the greatest benefit of the least advantaged" (the "difference principle"), but they must first be "attached to offices and positions open to all under conditions of fair equality of opportunity" (302).

Before one could attempt to determine whether the principles above are indeed likely to be chosen in the original position, it would seem necessary that their terms be defined so as to clarify the numerous ambiguities and indicate how the apparent inconsistencies among the principles can be reconciled. Among the difficulties that the bare statement of these principles raises are the following: Which liberties are basic, and why? Basic to what? How can the liberties to do different things be measured, added, and weighed against one another, in the absence of any standard except liberty itself? In cases of conflict, is it more important that liberties be "extensive" or "equal"? Furthermore, how are liberties to be defined so as to distinguish them from the social and economic goods in which inequality is allowable under the difference principle? Also, do not social and economic advantages necessarily increase one's opportunity (or that of one's heirs) to acquire further advantages—in violation of the priority of fair equality of opportunity to the difference principle? And what, precisely, *is* fair equality of opportunity?

Rawls makes no attempt to clarify any of these points before arguing that his two principles would in fact be chosen in the original position. What this omission demonstrates, I believe, is that Rawls is reluctant, or unable, to take his own notion of the original position seriously as a basis for determining or testing the principles of justice. To the extent that he provides any ground for choosing his two principles, this ground has nothing to do with any analysis of what a group of free, rational, equal persons such as he has described would be likely to agree upon. The choice appears rather to be the result of Rawls's selective lifting of the veil of ignorance and his creation of new, arbitrary conditions that determine the choice as a matter of definition—even while conflicting with the conditions he has previously laid down.

Let us first consider Rawls's purported justification of the priority of the principle of equal liberty, which "forbids exchanges between basic liberties and economic and social benefits," over the difference principle. Rawls explains that

the idea underlying this ordering is that if the parties assume that their basic liberties can be effectively exercised, they will not exchange a lesser liberty for an improvement in economic well-being. It is only when social conditions do not allow the effective establishment of these rights that one can concede their limitation; and these restrictions can be granted only to the extent that they are necessary to prepare the way for a free society.... Thus in adopting a serial order [i.e., the priority of the first principle to the second], we are in effect making a special assumption in the original position, namely that the parties know that the conditions of their society, whatever they are, admit the effective realization of the equal liberties. [151–52]

Several comments on this text are in order. In the first place, since Rawls has not yet specified what the basic liberties are (nor does he ever do so clearly or systematically), nor what they are basic for, it is impossible to determine what would constitute an effective realization of them, let alone the special conditions on which such a realization might depend.[8] Second, the statement seems to be a clear violation of the principle that the parties to the original position are not to choose in the light of any particular conception of the good. Rawls has now assumed *for* them that they will find equal liberty to be of greater value than any other good. Third, by making a "special assumption" about the parties' knowledge of the conditions of their society, Rawls has further violated the principle that they are not to know the particular facts about their society. We are entitled to ask why, if the parties are to be allowed this particular knowledge of their good, and of the circumstances of their society, they are not allowed to know, or at least investigate, the nature of the good and of the requirements of their particular society in other respects. The answer seems to be simply that Rawls wants them to have only the knowledge that will lead them to choose the principles he approves of. He can hardly claim sanction, then, for the priority of liberty as the outcome of the rational deliberation of free and equal persons: all he has shown is that he prefers it.

Similar things occur when Rawls attempts to support the two principles as a whole with "arguments . . . that are decisive from the standpoint of the original position." He presents these principles as "the maximin solution to the problem of social justice" (152). "The maximin rule," Rawls explains, "tells us to . . . adopt the alternative the worst outcome of which is superior to the worst outcomes of the others." It is "a conclusive argument" for the two principles that "the original position has been described so that it is rational for the parties to adopt the conservative attitude expressed by this rule" (152-53).

The original position as originally described by Rawls, however, did not point to such an attitude at all. One of the specifications for the veil of ignorance was that the parties were not to know the special features of their psychology, and hence their disposition towards risk taking (137, 172). Furthermore, while the maximin rule assumes that one's place in the society being designed will be determined by a "malevolent opponent" (152-53), and hence that one must expect, and prepare for, the worst in choosing principles for this society, Rawls had previously denied that the parties to the original position suffer from envy or other hostile feelings towards each other (144).[9]

Rawls explains the application of the maximin rule to the selection of principles of justice by providing a hypothetical "gain-and-loss table" of alternative choices. Since the parties to the original position lack knowledge of their conceptions of the good and hence of their utility schedules, however, gains and losses cannot be determined with reference to each party's overall utility. Rather, the entries in the table represent only *monetary* values, which Rawls here allows to represent all "primary goods" (153, 155).

The substitution of monetary values for general utility schedules only obscures rather than resolves the fundamental difficulty here. If the parties' ignorance of their utility schedule prevents them from weighing alternatives in the light of their overall utility (rather than of their gain in money alone), how can they know enough about their preferences to know that they prefer to follow the "conservative attitude" expressed by the maximin rule? Rawls has failed to show anything in the nature of rationality *per se* that dictates the adoption of the maximin rule in this or in any other situation. Quite the contrary: given the purely instrumental meaning Rawls has assigned to rationality, the preferences of the wildest of gamblers must be accorded an equal claim to rationality with those of the most conservative decision-maker. Rawls's own preference for the maximin rule appears to represent nothing more than a personal timidity. Surely he cannot claim, in the name of justice alone, the right to impose this attitude on humanity as a whole.

Rather than trying to meet this difficulty squarely, Rawls chooses instead to add further assumptions about the character of the alternatives facing his hypothetical decision makers that violate the condition of the veil of ignorance, and that are also unsupported by any reference to reality. He arbitrarily assumes that if a satisfactory minimum can be guaranteed through the two principles, there is "little reason for trying to do better," because "the person choosing has a conception of the good such that he cares very little, if anything, for what he might gain above the minimum stipend that he can, in fact, be sure of by following the maximin rule" (154, 156). Rawls has told us nothing of what would constitute a satisfactory minimum, or by what criteria it is to be determined, since it would be impossible for him to answer these questions in the absence of a substantive determination of the human good. Thus the statement that there is little reason to do better in such a case is hardly more than an uninformative tautology. And like Rawls's assumption that the given social conditions "admit the effective realization of the equal liberties," to the extent that the statement is not a tautology, it is an entirely unjustified violation of the veil of ignorance.[10] Rawls further violates the veil by asserting the superiority of his two principles to other conceptions of justice on the ground that those other conceptions "may lead to institutions that the parties would find intolerable" (156). Since Rawls had excluded from the parties' consideration both the nature of the good life and the resources available in their particular society, there is no way of telling that his two principles would be any more likely than other conceptions to secure a satisfactory minimum for all individuals in a given society, or for that matter to any individual in any society. Similarly, Rawls has no ground for assuming that the inequalities which might be sanctioned by the utility principle for the sake of greater social benefits are in fact intolerable: he merely posits that they are, and infers that since "the two principles of justice . . . secure a satisfactory minimum, it seems unwise, if not irrational," not to choose these principles instead (156).[11]

One further difficulty with Rawls's treatment of the balancing of possible gains and losses in judging various principles needs to be brought out. Since the terms "gain" and "loss" are relative not only to each other but also to some previous state, it would seem necessary for one to know with some specificity the character of the condition that precedes the choice of principles, against which the gains and losses from potential choices are to be compared, if the account is to be intelligible. Hobbes, for example, provided such a description through his account of the state of nature. Rawls's description of the original position, on the other hand, gives no real account of what the relations among men in such a position would be like. Although he has assumed that the human cooperation which requires agreement on a conception of justice is both possible and necessary (126), he has not indicated how necessary it is or for what ends, or what the consequences of not agreeing to the establishment of some particular scheme, or any scheme, of just institutions would be to an individual. Thus he has not shown that every individual would gain from such an institution, even if it were acceptable to some or most of the others. Rawls has refused to consider what sanctions, if any, could compel a person to agree to the institution of principles of justice, because he has denied that either bargaining or the threat of sanctions is relevant to the determination of justice (134, 139). But this exclusion prevents Rawls from demonstrating, as Hobbes did, the primacy of the need for men to come to an agreement regardless of their particular interests or conceptions of the good.

Of course, it is really meaningless to speak of a possible conflict of interest or opinion preventing the parties to the original position from coming to an agreement, since the veil of ignorance prevents them from knowing what their beliefs and interests are. But this means, I submit, that the notion of a contract among free and equal persons is simply irrelevant to Rawls's choice of principles.[12] Rawls presents these principles as the outcome, not of any bargaining that takes place in the original position, but of the unanimous choice (140) of individuals whose ignorance of their particular faculties, wants, and opinions makes them for all practical purposes identical. That the notion of a plurality of persons choosing the principles of justice is superfluous is indicated in Rawls's discussion of the gain-and-loss table that determines the choice: "There is no one playing against the person making the decision" (153). In other words, the rationality of the choice of principles hinges not on the need to work out a contract with other individuals whose interests and demands partially conflict with one's own, but on the arbitrary assumptions Rawls has made about the likelihood and desirability of the gains and losses resulting from various choices.

If the notion of a contract is really superfluous to Rawls's argument, why has he employed it? In the first place, Rawls thinks of the different parties to the original position as representing a diverse set of conceptions of the good. But since these parties make their decisions in the absence of any knowledge of what their conceptions of the good are, this is not a real function at all. The more fundamental reason for Rawls's use of the contract metaphor is, I believe, a rhetorical one. As we have seen, Rawls wants to convince us that we are obligated to follow the principles of justice he has asserted because we can conceive of their being chosen by representatives of mankind in all its diversity who are fairly situated with respect to one another. But he has not shown this. There is a good reason why Rawls commonly refers to the decision makers in the original position as parties rather than human beings or men: these parties are not human beings at all. By virtue of the way in which Rawls has constructed them—lacking any conscious conception of their aims and beliefs, lacking such human passions as envy and concern for others' well being—they are unreal, purposeless, lifeless ciphers, unanimous only in their anonymity. Their decisions can no more represent men's interests than would the tape that constituted the unanimous decision of a convention of computers, each of which had been identically programmed to reason from arbitrary premises to dubious conclusions.

By excluding from the original position the parties' knowledge of their real interests so as to simplify "the bargaining problem" (140), Rawls has omitted to consider the claims that real human beings would assert in such a situation. To think that actual men would or should accept these principles merely because Rawls's non-existent representative man allegedly gains from them (80) is fantasy.

4

I have tried to show that the manner in which Rawls constructs his original position, and particularly his inclusion of a veil of ignorance, renders this device insufficient as a basis for establishing adequate or even meaningful principles of justice. Even though Rawls himself, as I have pointed out, does not really derive his account of justice from the original position, the defects of that device are not without their consequences for his theory. What the original position does, in fact, is to obscure certain fundamental issues that must be faced if one wishes to achieve a truly adequate account of justice. It is necessary to take note of these issues in order to understand fully the deficiency of the two principles themselves.

The most fundamental fact that Rawls's veil of ignorance conceals—evidently because Rawls is either unaware of it, or unable to face it—is that not all conceptions of the good are compatible, or even commensurable, with one another. This is obvious in the case of the irreconcilably opposed spiritual ideals of Rawls's saints and heroes. Not only would such persons' conceptions of the good—*and hence of the just*—inevitably come into conflict with one another, but both these types of conceptions of the good are directly discriminated against by Rawls's two principles, which aim to maximize the so-called primary goods at the expense, in effect, of such other goods as civic virtue or piety. The promotion of the latter sorts of good would require the restraint of men's liberty to do as they please and of the pursuit of wealth, which breeds materialism and selfishness. The only sorts of persons whose conceptions of the good would seem to be advanced by the two principles are men with the motivation of the parties to Rawls's original position: mutually disinterested beings who "know" that the greatest possible sum of money is good but not that such things as virtue, honor, or holiness are good.[13]

Thus Rawls's theory of primary goods, which plays such a crucial role in his account of justice, is *not* impartial among different conceptions of the good. Rawls becomes increasingly frank about this fact later in the book, after the two principles have supposedly been established. He admits to the intention of remolding men's desires in the light of a particular view of the human good (259), and to defining "an ideal of the person" which is to be encouraged without regard to any "prior standard of human excellence" (327). At the same time Rawls summarily dismisses the argument that obligations to God must take precedence over the obligation to follow his own principles as a view that it is "unnecessary . . . to argue against" (208), treats desires for things that these principles do not allow as of "no value" (261), and advises men who find that such principles are contrary to their particular well being that "their nature is their misfortune" (576).

But why should men who might avert such a grave misfortune by refusing to accept Rawls's two principles agree to them? And why should anyone who believes that humanity's attainment of excellence, or its carrying out of God's commands, requires a way of life different from that which Rawls's principles prescribe, subordinate his beliefs to Rawls's? Rawls, never directly facing these problems, simply replies that the priority of justice as revealed by men's sense of justice demands the subordination of all else to its dictates. But whose sense is this? Not that of a serious Christian, Jew, or Hindu; not that of Aristotle or Napoleon, or anyone who believes that men's natural deserts are unequal, or that men's obligations to God take precedence over any obligation to maximize the general stock of primary goods. Rawls's sense of justice embodies not a universal moral attitude, but only a particular political ideology that the author has presupposed.

To note the partiality of Rawls's two principles towards some views of the good rather than others is by no means to refute them: *any* conception of justice, I have tried to suggest, embodies some particular conception of what is good. But the effect of the veil of ignorance is to enable Rawls to *avoid owning up* to the particular view of the good his principles entail, and therefore to omit any reasoned defense of that conception. Herein is to be found the fundamental difference between the original position and the accounts of the state of nature employed by the great social contract thinkers whom Rawls purports to emulate.

In a passage quoted earlier Rawls indicates that he has tried to generalize the notion of a social contract and carry it "to a higher level of abstraction." In so doing he attempts to liberate this notion from a dependence on any particular conception of the natural human condition, apparently regarding the latter as irrelevant baggage. But the result is that instead of resting on a serious consideration of fundamental human needs and desires, Rawls's conception of justice is founded on nothing more than the thin air of his intuition.

It is of course not accidental that Rawls's sense of justice leads him in the direction of a contract conception of justice that presupposes men's equality of rights. As a citizen of a liberal democracy, Rawls presupposes the validity of the ethos of that regime (319). But that ethos was originally shaped by such social contract theorists as Hobbes, Locke, and Rousseau. These thinkers used the analysis of a non-political state in order to reveal what man would be like in his natural condition, i.e., one free from any merely conventional restraints on his desires. As a result they were enabled to demonstrate why government is necessary, and what form it should take in order to meet man's most fundamental needs. Far from being an innate, primary, or irreducible phenomenon, Rawls's sense of justice simply embodies a loose and popularized form of the teachings of the great social contract thinkers. By treating this sense as if it were primary, Rawls omits to examine critically the grounds on which his beliefs rest. In order to do this one would have to return to the writings of his far more thoughtful predecessors.

It is revealing that Rawls, in citing the models for his social contract argument, alludes to Locke, Rousseau, and Kant, but omits Hobbes, whose *"Leviathan* raises special problems" (11n.). Rawls does not explain what these problems are, but one has reason to suspect that they are connected not only to Hobbes's well known "absolutism" and his criticisms of democracy, but also to his seemingly bleak view of human nature. Nevertheless, it is in Hobbes's writings that one will find the frankest and most forthright exposition of the principles that underlie Rawls's own theory of primary goods. Rawls's preference for other social contract theorists over Hobbes, as well as the consequences Rawls purports to derive from the contract, demonstrates primarily that he is unaware of the degree to which Hobbes's successors shared his conception of the nature of men in society.[14]

By tracing the origin of justice to a contract, Rawls indicates his agreement with Hobbes that justice is not natural, i.e., not naturally good for the individual. Rawls expressly acknowledges the conventional foundation of justice by observing that an individual would be better off if "all others are required to act justly but . . . he is authorized to exempt himself as he pleases," than if he too were required to act justly (119). This notion that justice is only instrumentally good is, of course, in tension, not to say contradiction, with the priority that Rawls attributes to it.[15] Nonetheless, Rawls's theory of primary goods demonstrates his belief that it is things like wealth and power, combined with the freedom to use them as one wants—which Hobbes sums up under the term "power"[16]—that are *really* good for a man. In terming these goods objective, on the ground that they are necessary means to almost all human ends, Rawls emulates Hobbes's use of the lowest common denominator of men's desires as the foundation of public morality. But unlike Hobbes, Rawls provides no reason for accepting such an approach.

Precisely because he presupposes the validity of his society's ethos, which he attributes to a sense of justice, Rawls fails to recognize, as Hobbes did, the controversiality of that ethos. Hobbes was aware, as

Rawls is not, that different men's senses of justice are likely to conflict, and are inextricably bound to their varying conceptions of what is good. Hobbes knew that it would be impossible to persuade men to agree on a particular conception of justice that would supplant their diverse previous views without demonstrating that this conception is actually more conducive to their well being. Far from presuming the correctness of men's intuitive beliefs about justice, Hobbes challenged those beliefs in the light of a reasoned analysis of the nature of man and his situation in the universe. Hobbes's state of nature, like those of Locke and Rousseau, excludes what Hobbes believes are merely conventional, socially inculcated notions of the good and the just, so as to identify the truly natural direction of men's inclinations.[17] Rawls, on the contrary, excludes fundamental *natural* characteristics of human life, such as envy, for the sake of conforming to his purely conventional notion of a "moral point of view."

Rawls omits from the original position all the harsh facts about the human condition that Hobbes's state of nature makes prominent, because Rawls cannot accept principles of justice that dictate the need for a powerful sovereign to compel men to obey the law in order to avert the terrors of their natural state. Rather than relying on laws and punishments to enforce justice, Rawls chooses to trust to men's sense of justice to regulate their conduct. Indeed, in the "well-ordered society" that his principles presuppose, Rawls believes that "there would be no need for the penal law" to be actually enforced (315). As we shall see in the next chapter, Rawls is less concerned that men may violate the law too frequently than that they may not violate it often enough; the doctrine of civil disobedience that he constructs in part 2 is intended to avert this danger.

Rawls's entirely unsupported assumptions about the clarity, consistency, and power of men's sense of justice undermine the need for establishing a conception of justice at all. If all men possessed an innate sense of justice that not only enabled them to make reliable judgments of justice, but actually insured that they would act justly without any governmental coercion, it is hard to understand how any injustice could have arisen in the first place. Consequently, there would be no need for government, embodying a particular understanding of justice, to regulate men's conduct. In fact, it is a striking feature, not only of Rawls's abstract description of the original position, but of his principles of justice themselves, that they do not provide any clear justification for the institution of government. If the greatest equal liberty is the superordinate good, and if liberty can be restricted only for the sake of liberty, why should men accept any limitations on the liberty to do as they please? Rawls replies that consenting to some procedure for resolving disputes is surely preferable to no agreement at all (354). But if men's sense of justice has the power Rawls claims for it, why should they need to agree on such a procedure in advance? Why not rely on men to resolve their particular disputes justly and peaceably as they arise? Alternatively, even if Rawls retracts his assumptions about the sense of justice so that governmental force is necessary to insure the peaceful resolution of disputes, why should men prefer a lawful, peaceable, but limited liberty to an unlimited natural liberty? Hobbes was able to answer this question by pointing out the disastrous consequences of the state of nature, and inferring that the *security* of men's lives, if nothing else, is a more fundamental need of all men than a legally unchecked liberty of action. Thus Hobbes prescribed limits to liberty in the light of a conception of what is good for men, given their natures, and concluded that the principles of justice can be determined only in light of this good. But Rawls, who wishes to maintain the priority of the just to the good, and of liberty to all other goods, is thereby prevented from following Hobbes's line of reasoning. Thus he cannot show that men are obliged to agree either on his own principles of justice, or on any others.[18] And he cannot justify his presupposition that men should be regarded as fundamentally equal in desert.[19]

Why, in view of the unsatisfactory consequences of this doctrine, does Rawls insist so doggedly on the absolute priority of an undefined liberty to any other good, and on the independence of his conception of justice from any particular view of the good? Purportedly, as we have seen, the reason is that teleological theories that subordinate the right to the good entail the possibility that some men's rights will be sacrificed merely to advance the general utility. But since Rawls does not show that such consequences follow from the principles of Hobbes or later social contract philosophers,[20] this explanation does not suffice. The real reason, I believe, is that Rawls is unwilling or unable to defend the particular conception of the good that his principles of justice embody against alternative views of the good life; and, furthermore, that Rawls cannot show that his abstract principles are conducive even to those minimal conditions of individual happiness that the modern liberal state, following the teachings of Hobbes and Locke, aims to provide—let alone any more exalted conception of the good life. I shall elaborate these deficiencies of Rawls's account of justice in the next chapter.

3

JUST INSTITUTIONS

And God saw all that He had made, and found it very good.

Exodus, 1.31

The arbitrariness of the world must be corrected. . . .

Rawls

I cannot stand forward, and give praise or blame to any thing which relates to human actions, and human concerns, on a simple view of the object, as it stands stripped of every relation, in all the nakedness of metaphysical abstraction. Circumstances (which with some gentlemen pass for nothing) give in reality to every political principle its distinguishing colour, and discriminating effect. The circumstances are what render every civil and political scheme beneficial or noxious to mankind.

Burke, *Reflections on the Revolution in France*

1

The purpose of part 2 of *A Theory of Justice* is "to illustrate the content of the principles of justice" that Rawls has purportedly established in the preceding section, "by describing a basic structure [of political and economic institutions] that satisfies these principles and by examining the duties and obligations to which they give rise." Although "the main institutions of this structure are those of a constitutional democracy,"

Rawls does not contend "that these arrangements are the only ones that are just." As we shall see later, radically different sorts of regime are in fact compatible with Rawls's two principles. The object of his account of a just constitutional democracy is "rather . . . to show that the principles of justice, which so far have been discussed in abstraction from institutional forms, define a workable political conception, and are a reasonable approximation to and extension of our considered judgments" (195).

Rawls begins part 2 by describing a four-stage sequence in which the practical implications of the two principles are to be elucidated. Each stage in the series represents a greater level of particularity in the decisions being made, and a consequently less stringent imposition of the veil of ignorance. In distinguishing these stages Rawls tacitly assumes that it is possible, at least in thought, to isolate completely decisions about which principles are just from decisions about what sorts of institutions are actually feasible. Thus only after the first stage (the original position in which the two principles of justice were established) has been completed is a hypothetical constitutional convention to "decide upon the justice of political forms" in light of those principles and choose a constitution with a view to securing the maximum equal liberty that, as the first principle asserts, is the most fundamental requirement of justice (196, 199). Although the delegates to this convention, unlike the parties to the original position, are allowed "to know the relevant general facts about their society," they are not permitted to question the previously agreed upon principles of justice in light of those facts (let alone in light of their conceptions of the good, of which they are still kept ignorant). Rather, their task is simply "by running through the feasible just constitutions" (i.e., those that secure "the liberties of equal citizenship," including "liberty of conscience, freedom of thought, liberty of the person, and equal political rights"), to settle upon the one constitution "that in the existing circumstances will most probably result in effective and just social arrangements" (197–98). While Rawls's language here suggests a distinction between a constitution's being just and its being effective or feasible, he apparently assumes that in all cases some constitution conforming to his definition of justice will also be feasible; it is this assumption which enables him to postpone the determination of feasibility until *after* the principles of justice have been agreed upon.[1]

Once a particular constitution has been chosen, it is to provide the rules "for reconciling conflicting opinions of justice" at the third or legislative stage, where "representative legislator[s] " enact "social and economic policies . . . aimed [in accordance with Rawls's second principle] at maximizing the long-term expectations of the least advantaged under conditions of fair equality of opportunity, subject to the equal liberties being maintained" (196, 199). Again Rawls presupposes the possibility of completely severing decisions of principle from those involving particulars: his description of the political process specified by the constitution "as a machine which makes social decisions when the views of representatives and their constituents are fed into it" (196) allows no place for the particular blending of principle and circumstantial judgment that constitutes the essence of statesmanship. A similar kind of abstraction is implicit in Rawls's distinction of a fourth stage in which the policies agreed upon by legislators are to be applied to particular cases by judges and administrators and followed by the generality of citizens: Rawls gives no evidence of recognizing the inevitably political, policy-making character of administrative as well as judicial functions. Thus even though it is only at this last stage that the veil of ignorance is entirely lifted, Rawls assumes that a responsible administrator's or judge's knowledge of particulars should in no way cause him to question the legislative policies that have been adopted in accordance with constitutional principles that represent, in turn, the application to politics of the principles of justice. "Conclusions from these principles . . . override considerations of prudence . . ." (135); the only legitimate ground for questioning the justness of a policy comes, not from a prudential awareness of its consequences, but from a belief that it does not correspond to Rawls's principles.[2] Thus the extent of an individual citizen's obligation to obey the law can be determined only from a theoretical doctrine specifying "the grounds and limits of political duty and obligation" in light of the original position, i.e., in the full darkness about particulars that the veil of ignorance guarantees (199-200).

The division of political decision making into the sequence of stages described above is necessitated by Rawls's intention of establishing the priority of justice to the good, and consequently defining a concept of justice upon which men could supposedly agree despite the most extensive disagreement in their political judgments, their religious beliefs, or their conceptions of the good. Rawls seems to be aware that a limitation of men's minds by the application of a veil of ignorance at each stage prior to the last would be impossible to achieve in practice. Despite its lack of correspondence to reality, however, he intends his four-stage sequence as a model of the kind of reasoning upon which actual human beings should attempt to base their judgments of the justness of political institutions.

Rawls's conception of the four-stage sequence is open to each of the main objections that have already been raised regarding the first stage, the original position itself. This conception rests on wholly unexamined assumptions on Rawls's part regarding the separability of general from particular knowledge, and of justness from goodness and feasibility. Rawls's claim that the four-stage sequence is analogous to "the United States Constitution and its history" (196n.) disregards the fact that no veil of ignorance was ever adopted, or simulated, by the makers of that Constitution, or of any constitution or laws. In order to recognize the absurdity of this device, one need only imagine the response that a delegate to the 1787 convention would have elicited had he proposed it.

I hope to demonstrate in the remainder of this chapter that none of the stages of Rawls's four-stage sequence is any more capable of producing reasonable standards for governing political life than the first one, the original position, was. Rawls's exclusion from the minds of his constitution makers and lawmakers of critical knowledge of particular facts, as well as their conceptions of the good, I shall try to show, inevitably gives rise to a barren and politically destructive doctrinairism. Rawls can claim that the consequences of his two principles are just only because he ignores all real objections to them, and can make them seem meaningful only through a series of non sequiturs and unjustified assumptions about reality. Rawls's particular prescriptions for political institutions do not derive, as he contends, from the working out of the principles of rational choice, but simply express a variety of ideological preferences on Rawls's part that he fails to show to be meaningful, consistent, or salutary.

2

In accordance with the principle that the requirements of liberty must be prior to all other goods, Rawls aims to incorporate these requirements in a constitution which is to limit the determinations of legislators about how other primary goods are to be promoted. Thus chapter 5 of *A Theory of Justice,* which constitutes the first main section of part 2, is devoted to the description of a "workable" constitution that satisfies the first principle of justice by securing the equal liberties to which all men are entitled.

Rawls's assumption that the justness of a constitution can be sufficiently tested by examining its conformity to his first principle alone exemplifies a remarkably narrow notion of what a constitution is. His postponement to the legislative stage of the question of social and economic policies is evidently intended to conform to the currently fashionable belief that liberty is equally compatible with a variety of economic systems: i.e., that it is as compatible with socialism as with capitalism.[3] This, however, was not the belief of the framers of the American Constitution, who thought that there was an inextricable connection between economic liberty, including the right to own private property and to reap the fruits of one's labors, and political liberty.[4] Many advocates of socialism, on the other hand, would contend that only that system is compatible with a genuine liberty.[5] Both sides would insist that economic questions are fundamental to the choice of a constitution, and vice versa. Rawls, however, passes over this issue as if it did not exist; he does not even find it necessary to consider economic freedom as part of his treatment of liberty. Rawls believes that a constitution can be rationally chosen not only in the absence of a consideration of social and economic matters, but even without the constitution makers' knowing their conception of the good: a constitution is merely a set of "procedures for coping with diverse political views," as with diverse economic views (197). He can apparently conceive of no reason why anyone who lives under a constitution should ever wish to undermine it, regardless of how far the social and economic policies adopted in conformity with it may diverge from his own opinions, so long as it satisfies the formal principles of justice Rawls has specified.

Given the priority that Rawls attaches to liberty as the goal of a just constitution, and the sharp dichotomy he lays down between this end and other primary goods, it would seem that his first task in describing a satisfactory constitution must be to give a specific, substantive meaning to the term "liberty." Most surprisingly, however, Rawls does not think that such a definition is necessary. Rawls believes that he can "bypass the dispute about the meaning of liberty" because "this debate is not concerned with definitions at all, but rather with the relative values of the several liberties when they come into conflict" (201). "Fortunately, however," Rawls asserts, "we do not often have to assess the relative total importance of the different liberties" (230). His remarkable solution to the problem of resolving such conflicts as that between political liberty, understood as simple majoritarianism, and the protection of other liberties through constitutional restrictions on the majority will, is as follows:

Usually the way to proceed is to apply the principle of equal advantage in adjusting the complete system of freedom. We are not called upon either to abandon the principle of [political] participation entirely or to allow it unlimited sway. Instead, we should narrow or widen its extent up to the point where the danger to liberty from the marginal loss in control over those holding political power just balances the security of liberty gained by the greater use of constitutional devices. . . . It is a question of weighing against one another small variations in the extent and definition of the different liberties. The priority of liberty . . . allows although it does not require that some liberties, say those covered by the principle of participation, are less essential in that their main role is to protect the remaining freedoms. Different opinions about the value of the liberties will, of course, affect how different persons think the full scheme of freedom should be arranged. . . . Ideally these conflicts [among different liberties] will not occur and it should be possible, under favorable conditions anyway, to find a constitutional procedure that allows a sufficient scope for the value of participation without jeopardizing the other liberties. [230]

All that Rawls has managed to say about the relative importance of the different liberties and their compatibility with one another, in the most extensive discussion of the problem that he ever provides, is that he will ignore the question! This failure is not incidental, I believe, but is the necessary outcome of Rawls's very approach to the nature of justice. In attempting to maintain the priority of liberty to other goods, and in seeking to provide a definition of justice upon which men can agree despite their differing conceptions of the good, Rawls is forced to avoid defining liberty in terms of the uses to which it is put. But any agreement that Rawls can secure on the priority of liberty without providing such a definition is, as the quotation above indicates, a purely formal one, which gives us no guidance as to how institutions should be structured. In fact, Rawls dismisses such questions as how far majority rule should be constitutionally limited, or how far the successful working of constitutional mechanisms to protect certain liberties "presupposes certain underlying social conditions," as matters that "lie outside the theory of justice" (229). How far is Rawls's conception of substantive political philosophy, as he terms his enterprise (202), from the architectonic science, providing guidance to statesmen and citizens, of which Aristotle wrote!

Rawls grants at one point that liberty is meaningful only with reference to "what it is that [men] are free to do or not to do" (202). Yet he does not seem to realize that as a consequence of this fact, his general principle that "liberty can be restricted only for the sake of liberty" (302) is wholly meaningless. It remains meaningless even when Rawls limits it to liberties that are "basic" (204)—not only because he never systematically specifies which liberties are basic, and why, but also because the most fundamental conflicts are among the most basic liberties. Indeed, as I have noted in the previous chapter, Rawls's account of liberty is so vague that it leaves entirely unclear the distinction between liberty and the other goods to which it is supposed to be prior.

Taken in itself, Rawls's first principle is so vague that it points to no particular set of policies, and is equally compatible, for instance, with liberal democracy and Marxism (depending on the sense and importance that are given in each case to different *forms* of liberty). Rawls does attempt, however, to give a more specific account of what he has in mind, by providing a set of "arguments for an equal liberty of conscience." He "assume[s] that these arguments . . . can be generalized . . . to support the principle of equal liberty" as a whole (211), so that he can dispense with any attempt to demonstrate the need for other forms of liberty.

Rawls begins his discussion of equal liberty of conscience by presupposing its conclusion: he asserts, without reasoning or evidence, that "the question of equal liberty of conscience is settled. It is one of the fixed points of our considered judgments of justice" (206). As usual, Rawls seems to assume that the dictates of his own sense of justice represent the unanimous verdict of all rational men. He wants to indicate, however, how "the question of equal liberty of conscience . . . illustrates the nature of the argument for the principle of equal liberty" from the standpoint of the original position. His argument is simply this:

> . . . it seems evident that the parties [in the original position] must choose principles that secure the integrity of their religious and moral freedom. They do not know, of course, what their religious or moral convictions are, or what is the particular content of their moral or religious obligations as they interpret them. Indeed, they do not know that they think of themselves as having such obligations. . . . Further, the parties do not know how their religious or moral view fares in their society. . . . All they know is that they have obligations which they interpret in this way. . . . Now it seems that equal liberty of conscience is the only principle that the persons in the original position can acknowledge. They cannot take chances with their liberty by permitting the dominant religious or moral doctrine to persecute others if it wishes. [206-7]

It is not only persecution and suppression, however, that the principle of equal liberty of conscience as Rawls interprets it proscribes. "The state can favor no particular religion and no penalties or disabilities may be attached to any religious affiliation or lack thereof" (212). Moreover, since the parties in the original position "do not share a conception of the good" or "an agreed criterion of perfection," they cannot agree to allow government to regulate men's behavior so as to promote their excellence or perfection (327). Not even sexual relationships that are thought to be degrading and shameful can be restricted unless they "interfere with the basic liberties of others"; there are no duties to self in the name of which men might choose to be governed (248, 331).

We may leave aside the contradictoriness of this description of the original position—for instance, the fact that the parties "know . . . that they have obligations" even though "they do not know that they think of themselves as having" "moral or religious obligations." (What other kind of obligation does Rawls have in mind?) We may even ignore the question of how a "doctrine" could "persecute others" or even "wish" to do so. What we are left with is simply an untenable argument. Rawls has not shown at all that parties in the original position, even those who were ignorant of their specific religious or moral convictions, would opt for the principle of equal liberty as he interprets it. If they knew that they had religious or moral convictions at all, they would be likely to adopt the principle that *whatever* the true religion or morality is, men should be *governed in accordance* with it.

To this Rawls will reply that although the parties do not know what their religious and moral convictions are, they do know that there are differences among their respective convictions, and hence that the principle I have stated cannot be applied without violating the obligations that some have to their beliefs, or to their descendants who would share such beliefs. "An understanding of religious obligation and of philosophical and moral first principles shows that we cannot expect others to acquiesce in an inferior liberty. Much less can we ask them to recognize us [i.e., the adherents of a particular faith] as the proper interpreter of their religious duties or moral obligations" (208). In other words, since religious persons cannot allow those of differing faiths to interpret their obligations, all must instead agree to make *Rawls* the supreme and final interpreter of those obligations! But Rawls has in no way justified his claim to be such an interpreter. What philosophical and moral first principles Rawls has in mind, or whence they are derived, he does not specify. But there is no evident set of principles by which Rawls could demonstrate to a religious believer that one's obligation to protect others' equal liberty to be atheists takes precedence over his duty to God. Far from even trying to provide such a demonstration, Rawls merely asserts that "it is unnecessary . . . to argue against" a position based on divine law (208).

The speciousness of Rawls's claim that his view of justice is prior to or independent of any particular view of the good, any "particular interpretation of religious truth," and "any special metaphysical or philosophical doctrine" (214, 217) is fully manifest here. It is absurd for Rawls to claim that the principle of equal liberty of conscience as he states it is compatible with all moral and religious convictions. However Rawls may deny it, his doctrine certainly does "require that government view religious matters as indifferent" and does imply "that the criteria of excellence lack a rational basis" (212, 238). No one who believes a religion to be true can be indifferent about whether people obey it; nor, if one holds that there is an objective human excellence, can one justify prohibiting government from regulating men's conduct in accordance with it.[6] As I have noted in chapter 2, to teach that primary goods like wealth, but not such goods as holiness or natural perfection, are "objective" ones, is to inculcate the belief that it is the former, rather than the latter, that are truly worth pursuing. Rawls's teaching thus tends to promote a materialistic, self-seeking way of life for mankind in which neither morality nor religion is taken seriously. Regardless of whether or not the reader is a religious believer himself, he might reasonably doubt that a society based on such a teaching would be truly conducive to men's well being. Yet Rawls refuses to consider whether, as many great political philosophers and at least some of America's Founding Fathers believed, some sort of public support for religion—to say nothing of morality—is necessary to the preservation of a free regime.[7] It is simply ruled out by his definition of justice.

In assuming the primary importance of men's coming to an agreement rather than their pursuing a way of life that is in accordance with the commands of God or the requirements of their natural perfection, Rawls again follows Hobbes's line of reasoning. But Hobbes, unlike Rawls, knew that it would be impossible to demonstrate the primacy of the need for agreement over the claims of religion without giving men reason to believe that those claims, insofar as they conflict with the terms of the agreement, are false. He attempted to do so both by a reinterpretation of Scripture aimed at showing that it is compatible with the principle of absolute obedience to the civil sovereign, and by an epistemological teaching which suggests the impossibility of the kind of knowledge to which the adherents of revealed religion lay claim.

Rawls's doctrine of equal liberty of conscience is ultimately dependent (by way of such thinkers as Locke and Adam Smith) on Hobbes's teaching, even though he does not seem to realize it.[8] Merely denying that his argument rests on "skepticism in philosophy or indifference to religion" (214) does not make this denial correct. Of course, there are grounds other than a Hobbesian skepticism on which one might defend a reasonable principle of religious toleration and oppose overly zealous moral crusades.[9] But no ground other than an extreme moral and religious skepticism (if that) would support Rawls's doctrinaire demand that government regard the promotion of religion and human excellence as wholly outside the sphere of legitimate public concern and regulation.

Because Rawls fails to comprehend the nature of a truly serious religious belief, he also fails to take seriously the arguments of those who viewed religion as a fundamental political problem. Hence he dismisses out of hand Rousseau's belief "that people would find it impossible to live in peace with those whom they regarded as damned" as "not borne out by experience" (215). The experience Rawls has in mind is clearly that of a twentieth-century American, living in a society which has "solved" the religious problem by diverting men from the pursuit of heavenly goods to the quest after earthly ones. But this is a remarkably narrow perspective for one who deems himself a philosopher.[10]

3

While Rawls's view of the human good as the secure and untroubled pursuit of private pleasures follows directly from Hobbes's teaching, there is one important element of the theory of primary goods that seems to go beyond Hobbes, namely Rawls's demand that individuals enjoy an equality of political influence so as to secure the primary good of self-respect (221-25). This aspect of Rawls's teaching seems to reflect the influence of Rousseau. Rawls has not, however, considered the conditions that Rousseau pointed out are necessary for the attainment of this political equality, or realized their incompatibility with his Hobbesian principles.

In conformity with Rousseau's general political teaching, Rawls believes that an individual's self-respect and consequently his happiness are dependent on there being a fundamental equality of condition between himself and others, including political equality. Rousseau, however, recognized that a truly egalitarian, simply democratic regime could be maintained only in a small, frugal community, whose citizens participate directly in the making of laws and are patriotic, pious, and virtuous.[11] Far from admitting these conditions, we have seen, Rawls undermines them by setting forth principles of justice that deny to the government the authority to promote religion or educate its citizens to virtue, that direct it to promote a maximal increase in material wealth, and that dispense with any obligation on the part of the citizenry themselves to take a care for their own or each other's virtue and piety. The equal sanctity of each man's plan of life as asserted by Rawls's means "do your own thing and leave others alone." Were a community of such non-religious, amoral, self-seeking men to let itself be governed directly by the will of the majority, its lifespan would in all likelihood fall short of that of the ancient republics, the instability of which was decried in the *Federalist*.[12] Alternatively, however, if what Rawls has in mind (as he appears to) is a large, commercial republic in which the popular will is filtered through representatives and limited by a constitution and a system of checks and balances, and in which commercial prosperity makes up for the defect in strength caused by the people's lack of virtue, then he will have to resign himself to there being an inequality of status and political influence among the citizens. But Rawls is unwilling to accept this, either. While he wishes representatives to be more than "mere agents of their constituents" since their first responsibility is "to pass just and effective legislation" (227), his demands concerning the electoral structure of a just constitution show no evidence of reflection on how this end can be brought about. His precepts that political parties should "be autonomous with respect to private demands" and "must advance some conception of the public good" in order to win office; that each vote should have "approximately the same weight in determining the outcome of elections"; that gerrymandering should be prevented; and that representatives should "be responsive to the felt interests of the electorate" (222-27) could have been drawn from the program of a New York Reform Democratic Club in the early 1960s; certainly they are not derived from any evident philosophic reflection on how the end of substantive justice can be secured, nor do they show any awareness of the practical objections that might be raised concerning both the feasibility and the desirability of these proposals.[13] Having laid down these precepts, Rawls hastens to excuse himself from having to defend them by "emphasizing that our discussion is part of the theory of justice and must not be taken for a theory of the political system" (277). But how can one determine what a just political system would be without considering, empirically and rationally, the nature of politics? What entitles Rawls to call his proposals "an ideal arrangement . . . which defines a standard for judging actual institutions" (227)? Since Rawls has not at all demonstrated the likelihood that these proposals would lead to substantively "just and effective legislation," he has not justified their ideal status in any way.

In his treatment of political equality, as in other areas, Rawls's procedure is to lay down contradictory requirements allegedly drawn from a theory, to avoid considering the actual political problems and difficulties to which they give rise, and to imply that all departures from his contradictory principles, however necessary, are something less than just. We may observe further instances of this procedure in Rawls's application of his second principle of justice, the difference principle with its qualifications, to the problem of devising just institutions.

4

Rawls's second principle, we recall, specifies that "social and economic inequalities are to be arranged . . . to the greatest benefit of the least advantaged," subject to the proviso that they must be "attached to offices and positions open to all under conditions of fair equality of opportunity." Political inequalities are ruled out entirely, we have seen, on the ground that they violate the equality of political liberty that is to be protected by the first principle. Whether they can be so sharply distinguished from social and economic inequalities is open to question; but Rawls does not take up this question. Nor is it at all clear what Rawls means by social inequalities, or how they are to be controlled. His discussion of the second principle is limited almost exclusively to economic matters. Here, as elsewhere, we note the materialistic bias of Rawls's conception of the good.

The bizarre assumption upon which the difference principle rests is that "no one deserves his place in the distribution of natural assets" (311), and consequently that society must be dedicated to "nullif[ying] the accidents of natural endowment" as well as those of social circumstance in the distribution of political and economic advantage (15). Rawls appears to have derived his assumption about the undeservedness of natural assets from the philosophy of Kant. But he seems unaware of the *dependence* of this doctrine in Kant's thought on what he arbitrarily dismisses as its "metaphysical surroundings" (264). And the inference he derives from it about the purpose of society in fact contradicts Kant's notion of morality.

Kant's denial that natural capacities are deserved stems from his dichotomy between the realms of nature and of freedom. Given the purposelessly deterministic character that modern science apparently reveals nature to have, Kant argues, no natural talent or ability can entitle man, as individual or as species, to claim any true superiority to a mere stone. Insofar as man acts in accordance with his natural inclinations, he is determined by the same laws that gave the stone its nature. The one faculty which enables man to rise above the rest of nature, Kant believes, is his reason. By acting in accordance with the commands of morality as they are dictated by reason alone, man expresses his unique freedom from external determination. The purely rational, and hence free, character of morality is due to its *universality:* the fundamental principle of morality, the categorical imperative, is based, Kant contends, on the simple idea of man as a rational being and of the treatment that reason necessarily shows such a being to deserve. The political embodiment of the categorical imperative—Kant's model of the just society—is a state which recognizes men's equality as rational, moral beings by treating them impartially, i.e., by securing their equal *rights.*[14]

Rawls frequently employs Kantian phraseology to justify the command that men obey his principles of justice—e.g., he claims that by following these principles men "most fully reveal their independence from natural contingencies and social accident" (255). But this claim is entirely illegitimate, because Rawls has not even *attempted* to demonstrate that his principles are derivable from the dictates of a universal reason.[15] On the contrary, we have seen, he traces them to nothing more than a sense or intuition. There is no reason to believe that in following a non-rational sense, man transcends in any way the behavior of the irrational animals.

It is not only the ground but the content of Rawls's principles of justice that contradicts the Kantian morality. The difference principle directly violates the Kantian dictum that each man is an end in himself, entitled to have his fundamental rights respected equally with those of his fellows. A government which treated men equally would be obliged to protect each man's right to develop his talents and enjoy the fruit of his labors.[16] Rawls, on the contrary, treats what he calls the distribution of men's natural talents, including even their character, as a "collective asset" which is to be utilized for the special benefit of *one* class: the "least advantaged" (101, 103, 319). His aim is to equalize, not men's opportunities, but their *achievements:* "Institutions are ranked by how effectively they guarantee the conditions for all *equally to further their aims*" (97; emphasis added); and resources should be allocated "so as to improve the long-term expectation of the least favored" by nature, even at the expense of the more intelligent (101).

Rawls justifies the policies above by claiming "that undeserved inequalities call for redress," and that "since inequalities of birth and natural endowment are undeserved, these inequalities are somehow to be compensated for" (100). His aim is to treat men in accordance with his view of them as equal moral beings. But in treating men *unequally* so as to *make* them equal, on the assumption that each man's individual qualities are a "collective asset to which he has no moral claim," Rawls commits exactly the sin for which he reproached the utilitarian: failing "to take seriously the distinction between persons" (27). What constitutes the identity of a person is his nature. It is therefore nonsensical to assert, as Rawls does, that "everyone benefits when the difference principle is satisfied" because the representative man whose nature is unknown gains from it (80).

Whereas Kant aimed to show how man, by following the dictates of a morality derivable purely from reason, could *transcend* nature, Rawls's aim is to *transform* nature. But this aim rests on nothing more than Rawls's own fiat. From the Kantian principle that "no one deserves his natural assets," it does not follow that *other* men deserve the fruits of these assets *more* than he does.[17] Rawls's demand that the natural distribution of talents be redressed in no sense represents a respect for humanity as such. Rather, Rawls wishes to transform humanity into something evidently quite foreign to men's nature: a race of radically equal beings who, regardless of the differences among their native talents, achieve—so far as is possible—the same results.

Like all ideologues, Rawls is at his most abrupt when his ground is weakest. Thus he summarily dismisses the contention "that the person with greater natural endowments deserves those assets and the superior character that made their development possible," and hence "deserves the greater advantages that he could achieve with them," as "surely incorrect" because it conflicts with what "seems to be one of the fixed points of our considered judgments . . ." (103-4). "The notion of desert," Rawls asserts, "seems not to apply to these cases" (104). "Of course," as Rawls himself concedes, "none of this is strictly speaking an argument" (104). But it is the only argument he supplies in support of his view.

Far from representing the considered judgments of most people, Rawls's difference principle is so much in opposition to common sense that Rawls must strive to transform language itself in order to argue for it. Thus even though "there is a tendency for common sense to suppose that income and wealth, and the good things in life generally, should be distributed according to moral desert" (310), or, as in the above example, according to men's effort and ability, Rawls simply rejects this conception of desert (310). But what meaning, then, is the term "desert" to have? Answer: "A just scheme gives each person his due, that is, it allots to each what he is entitled to *as defined by the scheme itself*" (313; emphasis added). Rawls's wish, it appears, is to redefine the very term "desert" so that it will mean nothing other than "what accords with Rawls's two principles." Thus may he hope to secure his principles against any objection; but he can hardly claim to have solved the problem of justice.

In order to recognize the absurdity of Rawls's conception of desert, one need only raise the question of why, in his endeavor to redress nature's injustice, he stops at equalizing the distribution of goods among *human beings.* If no individual man deserves to enjoy the fruit of his talents and labors, why should the human race enjoy goods which the other animals, by virtue of their natures, do not? Should we not dedicate humanity to the service of the beasts, who were "unjustly" treated through nature's failure to give them the power of reason that men enjoy? Once Rawls has rejected both reason and nature as standards for determining an individual's desert, he has deprived himself of any ground upon which to reject such a proposition. All he can say is that his sense of justice does not require it.[18] But by such a method of argument, one can say anything.

The fact that Rawls has no ground for limiting the redistribution of goods to human beings as distinct from other living (or non-living) things demonstrates the futility of trying to found justice on the denial that men deserve their natures. Since justice necessarily entails some proportion between the goods to be distributed and the merit of persons receiving them, to deny that people deserve their own natures—i.e., that which constitutes them as distinct persons—is to undermine any ground for distinguishing justice from injustice.[19] The notion of compelling people to "earn" their own natures is a daydream rather than a meaningful thought, and is founded on an unconscious attribution to men of an existence prior to their having "acquired" their natures. Once one sets out to combat "the arbitrariness of the world" (141), one has no criterion left for distinguishing arbitrariness from non-arbitrariness—for the world, so far as reason can determine, comprises everything that there is. It is impossible for a human being to achieve the "Archimedean point"[20] outside the universe for which Rawls strives: such a perspective belongs to God alone. In purporting to lead men beyond the world, Rawls seeks to subject them, not to justice, but to his own fiat. And as I shall observe in the following section, Rawls himself is forced to retreat from this posture (albeit without acknowledging this retreat) when he tries to issue prescriptions for carrying out his difference principle in practice.

5

Given the arbitrary notion of desert on which it is based, one might well view with alarm the attempt to enforce Rawls's difference principle as the essence of tyranny. But Rawls himself, in describing a just system of political economy, *does not adhere* to that notion of desert. The reader who has considered what appear to be the radically levelling implications of the difference principle will be amazed by the *conventionality* of the consequences for policy that Rawls actually draws from it. His standard of a just political economy requires nothing more than a competitive market system, government sponsorship of education to promote "equal chances of education and culture *for persons similarly endowed and motivated,*" progressive taxation, and the guarantee of a "social minimum" through such devices as social security or a "negative income tax" (275; emphasis added). Education, then, is *not* to overcome men's natural inequalities, but to provide the equality of opportunity in which these inequalities can be most fully developed. But how can Rawls justify such a policy, in view of his previous assertions? Answer: "As I have defined it, the second principle only requires equal life prospects . . . for those *similarly endowed and motivated*" (301; emphasis added). As Rawls giveth, Rawls taketh away. But underlying this contradiction of his earlier treatment of desert is the sudden recognition that to carry out that line of reasoning might require the abolition of the family (74, 301, 511). One may applaud Rawls's scruples, if not his consistency, in refusing to advocate such a step.

If Rawls's proposals for education will not bring about the radical egalitarianism that he had led the reader to expect, there is no indication that his other prescriptions for political economy will bring men closer to this result, either. How large a weight should the egalitarian principle of need represented by the social minimum be given? An "appropriate" one (276). Tax policies should insure that "as far as possible inequalities founded on either" birth or intelligence "should satisfy the difference principle" and should not "exceed a certain limit." What limit? "Naturally, where this limit lies is a matter of political judgment guided by theory, good sense, and plain hunch, at least within a certain range. On this sort of question the theory of justice has nothing specific to say. Its aim is to formulate the principles that are to regulate the background institutions" (278).

But Rawls has formulated no meaningful principles; he has merely endorsed the policies of the modern welfare state as appealing to his sense of justice. The fact that he has furnished no standards by which one could determine whether an actual inequality is or is not unjust according to his principles does not prevent him, however, from taking the opportunity to denounce "the injustice of existing institutions" (279; cf. also 87, 226, 520). Like the difference principle itself, this kind of obiter dictum has helped to win Rawls's book a certain popularity among the chicly radical.[21] But Rawls's judgment of existing institutions is unsupported, and it would be impossible to show that such institutions, or *any* institutions, violate the difference principle as Rawls has stated it. The justness of an inequality supposedly depends on whether it benefits those who enjoy less than equal advantages; but Rawls's abstract conception of political philosophy saves him from having to investigate what things actually *are* beneficial to the least advantaged, or to anyone. As he acknowledges, his theory does not even imply that hereditary inequalities or a hierarchical class structure are necessarily unjust (300–2). "In theory the difference principle permits indefinitely large inequalities in return for small gains to the less favored . . ." (536). Rawls justifies the acceptance of inequalities in accordance with the difference principle by rhetorically asking, "If there are inequalities in the basic structure that work to make everyone better off in comparison with the benchmark of initial equality, why not permit them?" (151). Since the proposition is practically a tautology, it would be hard to object to it. What it abstracts from, however, as Rawls admits, is the human passion of envy, and the effect that extensive inequalities might have on everyone's attainment of the equality of self-respect to which Rawls believes they are entitled (143-44, 151, 181, 442). In applying the difference principle to the problem of defining a just political economy, in fact, Rawls arbitrarily avoided including self-respect in his calculations, even though he regards it as the most important primary good (92, 440).

What can justify Rawls's disregard of the problem of envy in defining just institutions? In the first place, we are told that "the difference principle . . . presupposes . . . a certain theory of social institutions. . . . It relies on the idea that in a competitive economy . . . with an open class system excessive inequalities will not be the rule. Given the distribution of natural assets and the laws of motivation, great disparities will not long persist" (158).

But Rawls neither specifies what the criterion of excessiveness is, nor in any way demonstrates the truth (or even indicates the source) of this theory. Contrary to Rawls's assumption, recent research has confirmed what philosophers like Locke already knew: that legal equality of opportunity (i.e., the elimination of fixed, hereditary classes) still allows considerable inequalities in income and wealth to persist among individuals.[22] And Rawls himself previously noted that "the principle of fair opportunity can be only imperfectly carried out, at least as long as the institution of the family exists" (74). If large inequalities produce envy, then Rawls has not found a way to overcome this problem. The fact that great disparities may not long persist among different *families* from one generation to another is not likely to mitigate the feelings of envy that individuals may experience towards those who are better off than they.

In denying that the application of the difference principle in the manner specified above will give rise to strong feelings of envy, Rawls argues further that because his "contract conception of justice supports the self-esteem of citizens" by viewing them as equally "deserving from a moral point of view" and insuring them political equality, "the less fortunate have no cause to consider themselves inferior and the public principles generally accepted underwrite their self-assurance" (536). Once again Rawls's approach is wholly abstract, and is contradicted by the nature of things. What actually happens in a democratic society where men's conditions and opportunities are relatively equal and primary goods are pursued, and the reason for it, was noted by that acute observer Alexis de Tocqueville:

One must not blind himself to the fact that *democratic institutions develop to a very high degree the sentiment of envy* in the human heart. This is not because they provide the means for everybody to rise to the level of everybody else but because these means are constantly proving inadequate in the hands of those using them. Democratic institutions awaken and flatter the passion for equality without ever being able to satisfy it entirely. This complete equality is always slipping through the people's fingers at the moment when they believe it attained, fleeing, as Pascal says, in an eternal flight; the people grow heated in search of this blessing, all the more precious because it is near enough to be seen but too far off to be tasted. They are excited by the chance and irritated by the uncertainty of success: the excitement is followed by weariness and then by bitterness. In that state anything which in any way transcends the people seems an obstacle to their desires, and they are tired by the sight of any superiority, however legitimate.[23]

. . . .

No matter how a people strives for it, all the conditions of life can never be perfectly equal. Even if, by misfortune, such an absolute dead level were attained, there would still be inequalities of intelligence which, coming directly from God, will ever escape the laws.

No matter, therefore, how democratic the social condition and political constitution of a people may be, one can be sure that each and every citizen will be aware of dominating positions near him, and it is a safe guess that he will always be looking doggedly just in that direction. When inequality is the general rule in society, the greatest inequalities attract no attention. *When everything is more or less level, the slightest variation is noticed. Hence the more equal men are, the more insatiable will be their longing for equality.*

. . . That is the reason for the strange melancholy often haunting inhabitants of democracies in the midst of abundance, and of that disgust with life sometimes gripping them in the midst of an easy and tranquil existence.[24]

As in his treatment of political equality, Rawls in the application of his difference principle has attempted to straddle two canoes that are headed in opposite directions: the Hobbesian-Lockean view of the good as the maximization of individuals' material prosperity through the development of talents (and therefore of inequalities), and the Rousseauean view which identifies the good and just society as one in which men are actually equal, and consequently in which the development of talents, individual differences, and wealth must be severely limited. To decide the relative merits of these two views is a most serious issue of political philosophy; but Rawls contributes nothing to its resolution. Like the recent New Left, he is unwilling to face the fact that his demands for equality and community on the one hand and for the promotion of material prosperity and individual freedom from restraint on the other are in conflict with one another.[25] Such a refusal to face the contradictions contained in one's opinions is the very opposite of Socratic dialectic.

6

It remains to complete this examination of Rawls's account of just institutions by considering the doctrine of civil disobedience that he sets forth in his chapter on "Duty and Obligation." Rawls makes no attempt to justify this doctrine by an analysis of the likely decision of the parties in the original position. Instead, he simply *asserts* that "when they adopt the majority principle the parties agree to put up with unjust laws only on certain conditions," and that it "could not have been within the meaning of the duty of justice in the original position" that the parties be "required to acquiesce in the denial of [their] own and others' basic liberties" (355). No clear definition of what the basic liberties are, what limitation of them constitutes a denial of liberty as opposed to a necessary and hence justifiable restraint, or how the different liberties are to be balanced against one another has been offered by Rawls. Nor has he demonstrated that, assuming his view of justice could be made consistent, anything approximating it is politically actualizable. Nonetheless, Rawls is confident that while "we submit our conduct to democratic authority only to the extent necessary to share equitably in the inevitable imperfections of a constitutional system," it is never necessary to deny men's basic liberties or to distribute "the burden of injustice" unevenly "over different groups in society" (355).

The consequence of this abstract view of things is a radically subjectivistic view of the obligations of citizenship that, if it were widely adopted, would be destructive of *any* regime, and that, for this reason, is not at all likely to be chosen by parties in a pre-political original position who are in any sense rational and aware of the realities of political life. Although Rawls concedes "that there is a limit on the extent to which civil disobedience can be engaged in without leading to a breakdown in respect for law" (374), his teaching would encourage disobedience whenever an individual feels that a basic liberty has been abridged (372), that his government's aims in a war are "sufficiently dubious" (381), or even that "the public decision concerning the level of savings" is wrong (296). Rawls evinces no recognition of the need for a regime to instill in its citizenry a loyalty that will lead them to make sacrifices and even risk their lives for their country; quite the contrary, "given the often predatory aims of state power, and the tendency of men to defer to their government's decision to wage war," Rawls finds that "a general willingness to resist the state's claims is all the more necessary" (382).

But what reason is there to believe that an individual citizen is on the average more likely to be right about whether a certain policy is justifiable than a properly constituted government would be? Indeed, by what standard is the citizen to determine whether the government's policies are sufficiently unjust to legitimize disobedience to the law? Rawls provides no substantive answer to either of these questions. He asserts that it is often clear that the basic liberties "are not being honored" (372). Even if this assertion were true, however, it would not be the question upon which the legitimation of disobedience must turn; the question is rather whether the deviation from Rawls's principles of justice is or is not necessary or justifiable *in the circumstances.* Rawls simply leaves such judgments "to intuition" (246). The only guidance that he provides for judging actual policies is meaninglessly formal: "A law or policy is sufficiently just . . . if, when we try to imagine how the ideal procedure [the decision of rational, objective, impartial legislators 'who are conscientiously trying to follow the principles of justice'] would work out, we conclude that most persons taking part in this procedure . . . would favor that law or policy" (357). Yet Rawls *denies* that even "if many rational persons were to try to simulate the conditions of the ideal procedure and conducted their reasoning and discussion accordingly, a large majority anyway would be almost certainly right" (358). It clearly follows, then, that different *individuals* who tried to imagine the outcome of an ideal procedure would come to different conclusions about it. Indeed, Rawls himself is unable to specify substantive criteria for judging the just policy in given circumstances: his reference to an ideal procedure is mere buck passing. In encouraging individuals to disobey the law whenever their guesses about the ideal procedure disagree with the government's, therefore, Rawls is promoting anarchy.

Underlying Rawls's doctrine of civil disobedience is a political psychology that, not being based on any serious observation of human nature, suffers from a gross ivory-tower naiveté. From the fact "that an injured minority is tempted to believe its claims are as strong as those of any other" (375), Rawls infers nothing about the disposition of men to believe that they have a just ground for disobeying the law even when such is not the case at all. In this theorist's fantastic vision, civil disobedience is simply "one of the stabilizing devices of a constitutional system, although by definition an illegal one" (383). To those who "may object to this theory of civil disobedience that it is unrealistic," Rawls responds that he has "*assumed* throughout that we have to do with a nearly just society" (386; emphasis added). He does not consider what the effect of widespread disobedience to law may be on the *perpetuation* of such a society. "The theory of justice has nothing specific to say about these practical considerations" (376). Rawls concludes his discussion of this subject by disclaiming all responsibility for its consequences: "If justified civil disobedience seems to threaten civic concord, the responsibility falls not upon those who protest but upon those whose abuse of authority and power justifies such opposition" (390-91). *Après moi, le déluge.*

Unlike the great political philosophers of the past, Rawls has wholly ignored the psychological factors that are necessary to the support of any regime, and has severely underestimated the difficulty of maintaining one that is reasonably just. He assumes that the main determinant of whether people will support a regime is the extent of its correspondence to the abstract standard of perfect justice that he has constructed. He nowhere demonstrates the general existence in men of a sense of justice having the strength and objectivity that he attributes to it. (Indeed, as I have noted, if all men possessed such a faculty, there would be no need for government at all.) Rawls does not take into account men's tendency to be biased judges in their own cases, and to demand more than their due; nor does he demonstrate that there is in men an innate love of mere equality, as opposed to a desire to acquire as much as they can at the expense of others.[26] Above all, Rawls fails to consider how the encouragement of disobedience to law may undermine that *reverence* for law that both ancient and modern political thinkers have held is essential to the maintenance of any regime, but most especially a free one.[27] For the maintenance of free institutions, Rawls places his faith in their "natural strength" (219); he makes no effort to explain the relative rarity in history of long-standing free regimes, let alone the utter absence of anything like his ideal society. Thus far does the severance of political philosophy from political fact take us.

If Rawls's view of the obligations of citizens is unrealistic and unfeasible, it is also a mockery of justice. Rawls's democrat is not one who assumes any obligation to abide by the decision of a democratic government, but merely "one who believes that a democratic constitution" is most likely to "yield just and effective legislation." (296). Since even in a democracy "the people may still decide wrongly," Rawls's democrat will not believe that there is anything "sacrosanct about the public decision" and will feel free to disobey it in the name of his own view of what justice requires—even while reaping all the benefits that accrue to him from other citizens' obedience to the law (296). Although Rawls denies that the injustice of a law is "in general, a sufficient reason for not adhering to it" unless it exceeds "certain limits of injustice," the determination of these limits in practice, we have seen, turns out to be for all intents and purposes a *subjective* one which need not take into account whether circumstances make a real improvement of things possible or whether one's act of disobedience is likely to make things worse rather than better. Thus the individual's obligation to obey the law of even a fundamentally just regime is hardly a serious one. In fact, Rawls denies that citizens generally, as opposed to elected and appointed officials, have *any* "political obligation, strictly speaking" (114). His reason for this denial seems to be that, since officials enjoy the privileges of office, they must act so as to justify this enjoyment; whereas ordinary citizens, being guaranteed only the equal privileges of citizenship to which their merely being alive entitles them, *do not owe anything* in return for these privileges.

The defect of this "theory of political obligation," like that of the other parts of Rawls's account of justice, lies in the author's failure to derive his principles from a realistic examination of the nature of political life. Had Rawls seriously considered, as Hobbes did, the *alternative* to the maintenance of civil society, he would have recognized that the citizens of any decent regime have much for which they can be said to be obligated to it. The actual alternative to the preservation of a civic order is not likely to resemble the original position from which Rawls claims to derive his principles: a mere state of non-decision among free and equal parties who are "mutually disinterested" and free from envy and hostile passions towards one another (127–28, 143–44, 151). Rather, such an alternative is likely to come far closer to the state of nature that Hobbes described—a condition of the "war of every man against every man" in which life is "solitary, poor, nasty, brutish and short." The ever-present danger of such a condition, or something approximating it, given the nature of men, constitutes a persuasive reason why citizens should be discouraged from disobeying laws with which they disagree, except under the gravest of circumstances—generally those in which a regime as a whole (such as the Communist and Nazi tyrannies of the present century) is so rotten as to deserve to be undermined by *any* form of resistance, "civil" or otherwise. One ought not to delude oneself or others into thinking that disobedience to the law is likely to serve as a stabilizing device in most circumstances: to disobey a law, even for the best of motives, is far more likely to weaken the fabric of law, and hence of the political order upon which any possibility of justice depends.[28]

4

THE MORALITY OF
THE LAST MAN

*No shepherd and one herd! Everybody wants the
same, everybody is the same: whoever feels different goes voluntarily into a madhouse.... "We
have invented happiness," say the last men, and they
blink.*

Nietzsche, *Thus Spoke Zarathustra*

Rawls, as we have seen, purports to have established his two principles
of justice without deriving them from any particular conception of the
good. This claim is necessitated in the first place by Rawls's belief that
justice must be prior to and superordinate over goodness in order to avert
the objectionable results that arise from teleological theories such as
utilitarianism and perfectionism, which interpret justice as that which
is conducive to the good. The need to make justice independent of any
particular conception of the good is also due to Rawls's substantive
understanding of justice, according to which a just society allows men an
equal liberty to pursue their various notions of goodness, without
limiting or guiding that pursuit except insofar as justice itself requires
such limitation.

I have already observed Rawls's failure to demonstrate that his conception of justice is in fact impartial among various conceptions of the
good. The purportedly objective theory of primary goods on which
Rawls's contract conception rests, I have suggested, actually embodies
a particular, materialistic notion of the human good that Rawls never
succeeds in justifying.

The first two parts of *A Theory of Justice* contain scant consideration of the nature of what is good for man, and the problems involved in determining it. Rawls himself recognizes, however, that his theory requires some such account for its completion. His derivation of the principles of justice has rested on what Rawls calls "the thin theory" of the good (396-97), i.e., the theory of primary goods. In part 3 of *A Theory of Justice*, however, having completed his account of the principles of justice and their practical political implications, Rawls observes that several further questions must be dealt with for which "a more comprehensive account of the good is essential" (397). Foremost among these is the problem of stability: i.e., the issue of whether a society that conformed to the two principles of justice could be expected to sustain itself over time. The positive resolution of this issue depends, Rawls suggests, on the congruence between justice, as he has defined it, and goodness (399). In other words, although justice was purportedly defined without reference to any particular view of the human good, it must be established ex post facto that justice as Rawls has defined it is in fact conducive to a man's good, if each man is to have a sufficient reason to act justly and to support a system of just institutions. The demonstration of this congruence between justice as fairness and the human good is the most important practical task of part 3, which is entitled "Ends."

Part 3 is divided into three groups of chapters, of which the first group is concerned with laying out a theory of what Rawls calls "Goodness as Rationality." This section of *A Theory of Justice* is perhaps the most abstract section of a very abstract book. Its central conclusion is most simply summed up in Rawls's remark that he has "defined a person's good as the successful execution of a rational plan of life" (433). "The rational plan for a person," Rawls elsewhere explains,

is the one . . . which he would choose with deliberative rationality. It is the plan that would be decided upon as the outcome of careful reflection in which the agent reviewed, in the light of all the relevant facts, what it would be like to carry out these plans and thereby ascertained the course of action that would best realize his more fundamental desires. [417]

"As things are," Rawls observes, no choice of a plan can fully meet this criterion of deliberative rationality, since "our knowledge of what will happen if we follow this or that plan is usually incomplete." Hence the possibility arises that a person's choice, even if made after the fullest possible deliberation, will prove to be "an unhappy one." Nonetheless, in such a case, Rawls assures the unfortunate soul, "a person is not to be faulted for any discrepancy between his apparent and his real good" (417). However unhappy he may be, such a person at least need not suffer the opprobrium of having failed to exercise deliberative rationality.

To anyone who had thought that the purpose of moral and political philosophy is to guide a man towards the attainment of genuine happiness, the foregoing discussion, of course, hardly provides much solace. What is significant about this account of the good is what it omits rather than what it includes. Rawls's definition of the good is entirely a *subjectivistic* one. As Rawls explains,

we can think of a person as being happy when he is in the way of a successful execution (more or less) of a rational plan of life drawn up under (more or less) favorable conditions, and he is reasonably confident that his plan can be carried through. Someone is happy when his plans are going well, his more important aspirations being fulfilled, and he feels sure that his good fortune will endure. Since plans which it is rational to adopt vary from person to person depending upon their endowments and circumstances, and the like, different individuals find their happiness in doing different things. [409] [1]

Not only is this definition of the good subjectivistic; it is also, as Rawls acknowledges, "purely formal" (424). This formality provides an insufficient basis for testing the proposition that justice as fairness is conducive to each person's good. In order to fulfill this aim, Rawls endeavors to supplement his definition of the good by "tak[ing] note of certain general facts" about human motivation (424).

Typically, Rawls finds it unnecessary to engage in any examination of "the general facts about human needs and abilities"; these facts "are perhaps clear enough" so that he can "assume that common sense knowledge suffices for our purposes here." He does, however, distinguish "the familiar values of personal affection and friendship, meaningful work and social cooperation, the pursuit of knowledge and the fashioning and contemplation of beautiful objects" from other sorts of goods on the ground that the former "are not only prominent in our rational plans but they can for the most part be advanced in a manner which justice permits." In other words, such values are less likely to be promoted by means of injustice than other goals like wealth and political power. Hence adopting a schoolmarmish tone as he frequently does in this section of the book, Rawls "single[s] out for special commendation" those goals that are characterized by social interdependency rather than conflict (425).

Rawls adds to the foregoing "fact" about human goods "a basic principle of motivation" which he terms the Aristotelian Principle (424). According to this principle, which Rawls believes is implied even though not explicitly stated in Aristotle's writings (426n.),

... other things equal, human beings enjoy the exercise of their realized capacities (their innate or trained abilities), and this enjoyment increases the more the capacity is realized, or the greater its complexity. The intuitive idea here is that human beings take more pleasure in doing something as they become more proficient at it, and of two activities they do equally well, they prefer the one calling on a larger repertoire of more intricate and subtle discriminations. [426]

Rawls finds the Aristotelian Principle plausible partly because "it appears to be susceptible of an evolutionary explanation. Natural selection must have favored creatures of whom this principle is true" (431). Rawls provides no evidence to support this interpretation of evolution, and a moment's consideration of the plenitude of one-celled organisms might cause an uncharitable reader to challenge it. But regardless of its scientific support, or lack thereof, Rawls believes that the Aristotelian Principle is also "borne out by many facts of everyday life, and by the behavior of children and some of the higher animals," such as monkeys (431, 423n.).

The Aristotelian Principle would seem to represent a hierarchical criterion for ranking the merit of different human activities, and hence a means of overcoming the relativity of Rawls's definition of the good. But this turns out not to be the case. As Rawls explains:

... imagine someone whose only pleasure is to count blades of grass in various geometrically shaped areas such as park squares and well-trimmed lawns. He is otherwise intelligent and actually possesses unusual skills, since he manages to survive by solving difficult mathematical problems for a fee. The definition of the good forces us to admit that the good for this man is indeed counting blades of grass. . . . I mention this fanciful case only to show that the correctness of the definition of a person's good in terms of the rational plan for him does not require the truth of the Aristotelian Principle. [432–33]

Considering its questionableness as well as the fact (demonstrated by Allan Bloom) that it represents a gross distortion of Aristotle,[2] one might wonder why if the Aristotelian Principle is not after all essential to the "definition of a person's good," Rawls has introduced or invented it at all. The answer is supplied, I believe, by Rawls's discussion of what he calls "perhaps the most important primary good . . . that of self-respect" (440).

Rawls "define[s] self-respect (or self-esteem) as having two aspects": "First of all, . . . it includes a person's sense of his own value, his secure conviction that his conception of his good, his plan of life, is worth carrying out. And second, self-respect implies a confidence in one's ability, so far as it is within one's power, to fulfill one's intentions" (440).

One of the critical arguments in favor of justice as fairness, according to Rawls, is that by treating men's desert as equal, it provides the necessary foundation for self-respect (440). An individual's self-respect is in Rawls's view utterly dependent on what others think of him: "Unless our endeavors are appreciated by our associates it is impossible for us to maintain the conviction that they are worthwhile" (441).[3] And it is here that the relevance of the Aristotelian Principle finally emerges. Even assuming that the application of the two principles of justice would assure to all men an equality of liberty, and an adequate parity in other primary goods, the self-respect of some might still be threatened if other men did not esteem their *activities* as much as they desired. Hence the Aristotelian Principle, properly interpreted, is needed as a remedy:

> The application of the Aristotelian Principle is always relative to the individual and therefore to his natural assets and particular situation. It normally suffices that for each person there is some association (one or more) to which he belongs and within which the activities that are rational for him are publicly affirmed by others. In this way we acquire a sense that what we do in everyday life is worthwhile. . . . Judged by the doctrine of perfectionism, the activities of many groups may not display a high degree of excellence. But no matter. What counts is that the internal life of these associations is suitably adjusted to the abilities and wants of those belonging to them, and provides a secure basis for the sense of worth of their members. The absolute level of achievement, even if it could be defined, is irrelevant. But in any case, as citizens we are to reject the standard of perfection as a political principle, and for the purposes of justice avoid any assessment of the relative value of one another's way of life. . . . This democracy in judging each other's aims is the foundation of self-respect in a well-ordered society. [441–42]

Rawls's egalitarianism here takes on a new dimension. The equality to which justice as fairness entitles men guarantees them not only an equality of liberties, and the allowance of inequalities in other primary goods only to benefit the least advantaged, but also an equality of esteem for their activities. We may understand the role of the Aristotelian Principle in advancing this goal as follows. The Aristotelian Principle is intended to account for men's choosing activities that involve "exercising the higher abilities" they possess (430), *without* thereby implying that such more complex activities are therefore qualitatively higher, nobler, or more worthy of esteem than others.[4] In other words, the fact that men tend to admire activities like philosophy and statesmanship more than others is merely a manifestation of the tendency, allegedly common to monkeys and children, to think that more complex pursuits are more choiceworthy. Interpreting such activities in this light ought to lead us to see that philosophy and politics do not *need* to be regarded as *objectively* superior to other pursuits—for instance, counting blades of grass. Hence it paves the way for adopting the "democracy in judging each other's aims" that is the prerequisite of a well-ordered society.

Rawls's entire account of the human good in part 3 is intended to advance this form of democracy. Rawls systematically denies the objective superiority of any activity that might be thought to make a man more worthy of admiration than his fellows. There is no intrinsic merit, according to Rawls, to participating actively in politics (227), to the process of deliberation (418), or to the attainment of truth (419). Those men such as Loyola (or, one might add, Socrates) who have single-mindedly devoted themselves to the pursuit of one transcendent goal that they thought infinitely more important and valuable than any other are, on Rawls's account, unhealthy or inhuman (553). A rational plan of life is rather one that "will include many (or at least several) final aims," thus satisfying "the desire for variety and novelty of experience" (549, 427).

One can see how professional grass counters might think they would gain from a system which guaranteed them an "equality in the social bases of esteem" (546) with Plato, Napoleon, and Jascha Heifetz. But what could possibly induce men of preeminent ability in what have widely been regarded as higher activities to agree to such a scheme?

Rawls's answer to this question is that, by accepting the universal democracy he has described, all men enable themselves to participate in the great good represented by the "idea of social union" (571, 520). Rawls contends that, "despite the individualistic features of justice as fairness"—particularly its derivation from an original position in which men are assumed to be isolated from social connections—this doctrine provides "a satisfactory framework for understanding the values of community" (520). In contrast to previous social contract theorists, Rawls holds that the nature of man is in fact radically social, and that the true realization of this sociality requires the obliteration of all barriers that separate and divide human beings from one another.

We need one another as partners in ways of life that are engaged in for their own sake, and the successes and enjoyments of others are necessary for and complimentary [*sic*] to our own good. . . . When men are secure in the enjoyment of their own powers, they are disposed to appreciate the perfections of others, especially when their several excellences have an agreed place in a form of life the aims of which all accept. Thus we may say . . . that it is through social union founded upon the needs and potentialities of its members that each person can participate in the total sum of the realized natural assets of the others. We are led to the notion of the community of humankind the members of which enjoy one another's excellences and individuality elicited by free institutions, and they recognize the good of each as an element in the complete activity the whole scheme of which is consented to and gives pleasure to all. This community may also be imagined to extend over time, and therefore in the history of a society the joint contributions of successive generations can be similarly conceived. [522–23]

Rawls's idea of social union constitutes the ultimate justification of his theory of justice, and at the same time is the means by which the acceptance of these principles is to be brought about. Rawls contends that each individual ought to agree to the two principles because they express the true nature of his self, i.e., that of "a free and equal moral person" whose "conception of the good as given by his rational plan is a subplan of the larger comprehensive plan that regulates the community as a social union of social unions" (565, 563). "... The desire to express our nature as a free and equal rational being can be fulfilled only by acting on the principles of right and justice" as Rawls has defined them, since acting from the precedence of principles that recognize all men's right to freedom and equality "expresses our freedom from contingency and happenstance" (574). Rawls believes that at present "the injustice of institutions and the often squalid behavior of others" obstruct the actualization of genuinely just human relations, because existing injustices serve as an excuse to the evildoer to justify his own misconduct. The establishment of a well-ordered society, however, will right this situation (570). It is through the moral education of mankind in such a society that men's present disposition to injustice will be overcome, thus practically eliminating the need for penal sanctions to be enforced (240, 576–77).

We have already observed that Rawls's project involves the remaking, not only of human society, but of human nature itself. Only in part 3, however, does the full extent of that project become apparent. By overcoming the "arbitrariness found in nature" (102), Rawls intends to give the self as he understands it "free reign" [sic] irrespective of "the contingencies and accidents of the world" (575). The realization of this goal requires that future human beings be molded in accordance with the dictates of the true principles of justice, rather than according to men's present desires and beliefs. "The long range aim of society" is to be "settled ... irrespective of the particular desires and needs of its present members" (261). Furthermore, "In justice as fairness one does not take men's propensities and inclinations as given, ... and then seek the best way to fulfill them. Rather, their desires and aspirations are restricted from the outset by the principles of justice which specify the boundaries that men's systems of ends respect" (231).

Since the purpose of just institutions is "to foster the virtue of justice and to discourage desires and aspirations incompatible with it" (261), Rawls ordains that all individuals should undergo a process of moral instruction to which he believes no one in a well-ordered society could object (515). While some might argue that what Rawls is proposing is a program of coercive indoctrination, he reassures them that this is not the case, since the principles they are to be taught are those "that they would acknowledge under conditions that best express their nature as free and equal rational beings" (515). Surely no right-thinking person should wish to satisfy desires that run contrary to the two principles of justice: there is "no value in fulfilling" such desires, and they consequently "have no weight" (261). Justice, as Rawls understands it, is uncompromising (4). Consequently, while lamenting that "as things are, legislators must reckon with strong public feelings" (231), Rawls looks forward to a situation where this will no longer be a problem.[5] In a well-ordered society, there will be no disagreement about the meaning of justice (5), and "no questions [will be] asked" about the substantive justness of an existing distribution of goods (94).

For all his purportedly liberal intentions, we see that Rawls is finally driven, in advancing his project, to adopt the language of tyranny. By no means short of a tyranny could anyone hope to institute a social order irrespective of its present members' desires and needs, or dismiss desires for unjust things as defined by Rawls's scheme—such as the desire for more social esteem than other men receive—as of no value, and thereby prevent them from being satisfied. Rawls's endeavor to reconstitute society in utter disregard of its present members' desires and beliefs recalls Socrates' ironic account of the first step a philosophic ruler would take in constituting a just city: the expulsion of all inhabitants over the age of ten.[6] But Rawls is serious.

The tyrannical tendency implicit in the remarks just quoted compels us to question the depth of Rawls's professed commitment to liberty. Rawls claims, as we have seen, that his first principle of justice gives liberty a priority over all other goods. Yet if justice is said to dictate that the fundamental structure of society be constituted without reference to the wishes of its present members, and to require that everyone's nature be remolded so as to lead to the acceptance of the two principles of justice, the actual scope of liberty appears to be severely circumscribed. In retrospect, it appears that such circumscription of liberty is acceptable to Rawls because he regards liberty—despite its supposed priority—as valuable primarily as a *means* to other, ill-defined goals, rather than as intrinsically choiceworthy. At one point in part 2 Rawls describes "the worth of liberty to persons and groups" as being "proportional to their capacity to advance their ends . . ." (204). Further on, he elaborates that the "fair value of political liberty" in particular depends on how much property and wealth one possesses (226). If this is true, then it would make sense to constrain men's liberty for the sake of other goals to which it is instrumental and subordinate.

But what goal, then, is Rawls's ultimate standard of value? Rawls has steadfastly denied that liberty can justly be sacrificed for the sake of such other primary goods as wealth. Yet his wish to dogmatically impose the two principles of justice on men regardless of their actual opinions and desires, and his recommendation that men be remolded so as to accord with these principles, obviously involve a considerable limitation of liberty. On what ground is this limitation to be justified?

The answer to this question, it seems, is that the ultimate good for Rawls is self-respect, which (as we have seen) he believes to be entirely dependent on the actualization of what he calls the idea of social union. It is of far greater importance to every man, according to Rawls, for the individual to acquire "a secure basis for the sense of [his] worth" (442) through membership in a true social union with all others, even if this requires some sacrifice of primary goods *including liberty,* than that an increase in the latter should be purchased at the expense of the former. Here, then, is Rawls's response to Glaucon's charge, in Plato's *Republic,* that a superior man would benefit more from a life of successful injustice than one of justice: by so living, he would deprive himself of "the values of community" with other men through which "the self is realized" (565). Moreover,

> . . . a person . . . who would never act as justice requires except as self-interest and expediency prompt, not only is without ties of friendship, affection, and mutual trust, but is incapable of experiencing resentment and indignation. . . . Put another way, one who lacks a sense of justice lacks certain fundamental attitudes and capacities included under the notion of humanity. Now the moral feelings are admittedly unpleasant . . . ; but there is no way for us to avoid a liability to them without disfiguring ourselves. [488–89]

Let us grant Rawls that self-respect is the most fundamental component of human happiness and well being. His reply to Glaucon then depends on several premises, each of which stands in need of elaboration and demonstration: first, that a fully developed man's self-respect is entirely dependent on what others think of him; second, that this self-respect is similarly dependent on his participation in the kind of social union sketched by Rawls; third, that a man who acts unjustly is in fact incapable of enjoying friendship or experiencing indignation; and fourth, that justice is best represented by Rawls's two principles. Unfortunately, Rawls never provides a suitable elaboration of any of these premises. And each of them is either highly questionable or radically defective.

Let us begin by reexamining Rawls's understanding of self-respect and its preconditions. Consider, first, the following definition of self-respect, provided by the *Oxford English Dictionary:* "proper regard for the dignity of one's person or one's position." Self-respect is linked by this definition to dignity, which is defined in the same work as "the quality of being worthy or honourable; worth, excellence; desert."

The view of self-respect that is summarized by these definitions conforms, I believe, to men's ordinary understanding of the term. To respect oneself is to think oneself good, worthy, and honorable. Human beings are the only living creatures capable of feeling self-respect, because this feeling is dependent on the uniquely human faculty of judging and evaluating. Whether he likes it or not, no man can avoid judging himself. It is in fact on the ground of this human faculty for self-judgment that Aristotle founds his definition of happiness, according to which man is the only animal that is capable of experiencing happiness, as opposed to mere pleasure. Whereas pleasure is temporary, and may be produced by simple physical sensation, happiness is by definition continuous (although not necessarily permanent). To be happy is to be in a good state or condition, and to be *cognizant* of one's goodness.[7] Self-respect or self-approbation is indeed, as Rawls recognizes, the core of happiness. However many pleasures he may experience, no man can be happy who does not respect himself. It is for this reason that even wealthy, famous, and powerful men, whose position others envy, may nonetheless be unhappy, while the poor and infamous Socrates enjoyed a happiness that was largely independent of the commonly desired external goods. For the same reason, men may despise themselves for indulging in pleasures to which their physical nature impels them "in spite of themselves." The capacity for self-respect and consequently for self-judgment is a reflection of the duality of human nature, which enables man in a sense to stand outside himself and to judge independently the merit of the activities in which he is engaged and the life he leads.

Just as Rawls is correct in identifying self-respect as the most important primary good, so he rightly observes that men's self-respect is *ordinarily* connected to their awareness of how they are regarded by their fellows. Because of man's social nature, he cannot avoid comparing himself with others; only with great difficulty, moreover, can he avoid letting his self-estimation be influenced by the way that others compare themselves with him. Perhaps the profoundest analysis of this faculty of self-comparison was set forth by Jean-Jacques Rousseau, who explains it as one of the two fundamental forms of self-love (*amour-propre* as distinguished from *amour de soi*). Rousseau finds *amour-propre*—the desire to be esteemed by others to the same degree that one esteems oneself—to be the source both of men's greatest virtues and of their greatest vices. *Amour-propre* is, according to Rousseau, the root of men's pursuit of all goods that go beyond the "necessary" ones—i.e., those necessary for the mere maintenance of life, with which the other animals content themselves. *Amour-propre* stimulates men to compete for such varied goals as love, wealth, political power, and artistic achievement—in each case, not primarily because of the innate or natural attractiveness of these goals considered in themselves, but rather for the sake of earning other men's admiration, and hence enhancing one's own self-respect.[8]

For Rousseau the fact of *amour-propre* constitutes the essence of the human problem—a problem to which no simple or complete solution is possible. The impossibility of such a solution is due to the ambiguity of the effects of *amour-propre,* which according to Rousseau are beneficial to the few who achieve greatness as a result of their quest for admiration, but harmful to the many who are thereby rendered subordinate and inferior. Rousseau's best-known solution to this problem for the sake of the many is set forth in the *Social Contract,* which describes a republican regime based on the principle of civic virtue in which all the citizens could enjoy a sense of equal freedom through their participation in self-government. The incompleteness of this solution, however, can most simply be indicated by noting that it provides no place for a man with the unique gifts of Rousseau himself.[9]

What is problematic to Rousseau—and to every serious thinker who ever concerned himself with this issue—is remarkably unproblematic to Rawls. As we noted in chapter 3, Rawls believes he can secure the good of community, and the support it provides to men's self-respect, *without* maintaining any of the conditions Rousseau thought were the prerequisites of such community (civil religion, limitations on luxury, active citizen participation in government, and so on). Nor does Rawls seem to recognize that there is any necessary connection between feeling self-respect and having an objective *reason* for feeling it. Merely by pronouncing it just to give all men an "equality in the social bases of esteem," and promising men a participation in "the good of social union" in return, Rawls thinks he can persuade his readers that they *should* esteem all men equally, regardless of differences in their character, abilities, or achievements.

Rawls tries to sanctify his vision of universal, equal social esteem by reverting to the language of Kant—as in his claim that obeying the two principles of justice expresses men's freedom from "the contingencies and accidents of the world" (575). But this is a grave misuse of Kant.[10] While teaching that one should act so as to regard each man as an end in himself, Kant did not infer that we are obliged to esteem each man's *achievements* equally—putting the work of Plato and Rawls's hypothetical grass counter, for instance, on the same evaluative plane.

Moreover, the transference of a Kantian halo to Rawls's conception of justice is belied, as several commentators have pointed out, by the contractuarian derivation of Rawls's conception, which he naively wishes the reader to forget (116).[11] As previously noted, Rawls's derivation of justice from a contract was based on the assumption that a deference to other men's claims is not naturally good for an individual, but that each man would be best off with the liberty to do as he pleases, and with the greatest possible stock of other primary goods. In sum, so long as he was engaged in constructing the principles of justice, Rawls agreed with Glaucon and Hobbes that justice—far from being the greatest good—is at best a compromise among men's competing interests (119). Yet, once having determined the two principles in the light of this assumption, Rawls wishes to call his artificially conceived justice "a natural duty," and uses it "to define an ideal of the person" that is nonetheless ungrounded in any natural standard of human excellence (115, 327). The radical disjunction between the concept of goodness that Rawls employs to justify men's obligation to justice as he defines it and the concept of goodness that he used in deriving the principles of justice is made manifest by his description of the virtues as "properties that it is rational for persons to want *in one another*" and "a good act" as one that promotes "another's good" (404, 438; emphasis added). These quotations tacitly concede that it is not in fact advantageous for an individual himself to be good or just in Rawls's sense; and no wonder, for the morality Rawls laid down was contrived so as to maximize the gains of others in terms of their "objective," primary goods. In other words, the justice that Rawls calls good is not really good for the man who practices it, but benefits only those towards whom it is practiced.

It is impossible to reconcile a contract conception of justice, which presupposes that it is only instrumentally good, with the claim that justice is a transcendent good having priority over particular individual interests. Had Rawls truly believed the latter claim, he would have had to construct an account of the just society that was aimed at inculcating a just and public-spirited character in men, by directing them *away* from the pursuit of primary goods other than self respect. As things stand, Rawls's assertions about the "good of justice" in part 3 constitute an intellectual sleight-of-hand that is morally blameless only because Rawls himself appears to be genuinely unaware of it.

The underlying intention of Rawls's account of justice—which he seems unable to acknowledge to himself, any more than admit it to his readers— is to enslave men of superior talent or industry to the service of the least advantaged, by convincing *them* that it is good to be just in his sense—even though the theory of primary goods implicitly denies this. Rawls's wish to subjugate the few to the many is so strong that in the end it entirely over-comes his professed commitment to individual liberty. In his notion of the self as a free and equal moral person which "is the same for all," "is realized in the activities of many selves," and forms part of a community through which men "participate in one another's nature" (565), Rawls surpasses with utter seriousness even that communization of the individual that was ironically proposed by Socrates in the *Republic*. Yet Rawls's "social union of social unions" is not intended, as the community of the *Republic* is, to promote the perfection of man's nature, but serves to maximize only the expectations of the non-existent representative man, who "represents" only the lowest common denominator of men's desires. No genuine community among actual human beings can be established on such a basis.

The true model for Rawls's radically egalitarian morality is to be found neither in Rousseau, Kant, nor Plato, but rather in Friedrich Nietzsche's scornful portrait of what he calls "the last man."[12] The member of Rawls's just society, like the last man, is a totally socialized being, homo-geneous with his fellows, without any serious commitments, who seeks merely to while away his life in idle and easy pastimes and yet demands that all others esteem him for this.[13] Wanting a society that will make him feel comfortable and secure and otherwise leave him alone, Rawlsian man seeks a world in which there will be, to use the words of Nietzsche's Zarathustra, "no shepherd and one herd." Despite its pretense to freedom, such a society is not really free. Like Marx's vision of communist society, it requires the tyrannical remolding of human nature so as to close off all human possibilities except that of being a last man—a being who is devoid of all those qualities that make man distinctively human.[14]

Far from being liberal in any genuine sense, Rawls's conception of justice, as elaborated in part 3, would be disastrous for liberal society if it were adopted. Modern liberalism rests on the supposition that men, if allowed liberty and opportunity to exercise their talents in behalf of their respective interests, will have a powerful motive to develop them, and therefore indirectly to benefit society as a whole.[15] Precisely because they know that the esteem they desire can be acquired only by earning it, they will have perhaps the strongest of incentives to better themselves. But at the same time, because the role of government in regulating men's lives is limited, there will be an opportunity for men who think differently from others to pursue the truth independently of what their fellows believe—without thereby risking the fate of Socrates.

His professions to the contrary notwithstanding, Rawls severely denigrates liberty. Although liberty in the just society is to be equal among the members of that society, Rawls himself stands outside and above this system, constraining the freedom of the equal citizenry and determining its content in the name of what he considers to be "the nature of the self as a free and equal moral person" (565).

As Allan Bloom has written, Rawls "owes us and himself a fuller account of the 'self'" than he provides.[16] The self as Rawls describes it is barely more deserving of the title "human" than were the artificially conceived parties to the original position. Man as Rawls conceives him is lacking in the most fundamental form of freedom because his self-conception is *entirely* derived from the way that others regard him. In other words, there is no possibility for a man to think differently from the herd.

As I have noted, there is an evident tendency for men to be *influenced* in their self-conception by what other men think of them. But sensible men at least make a distinction among *whose* opinions they respect: the opinions of children, flatterers, and fools are obviously not to be regarded in comparison with those of wise and good men. Moreover, it is the mark of a truly mature human being to develop his own internal standards of praise and blame, having a certain independence from what the majority of men say and do. The nature of what one may call a genuine self-esteem or pride is beautifully illustrated by a story Booker T. Washington tells of the response made by another great black leader, Frederick Douglass, to the imposition of racial segregation in the American South. Upon receiving apologies from some white sympathizers for having been degraded by being forced to ride in the baggage car of a train, "Mr. Douglass straightened himself up on the box upon which he was sitting, and replied: 'They cannot degrade Frederick Douglass. The soul that is within me no man can degrade. I am not the one that is being degraded on account of this treatment, but those who are inflicting it upon me.'"[17]

The notion of such an *independent* sense of self-worth is entirely foreign to Rawls's conception of man. One suspects that Rawls would not wish to encourage such independence, precisely because men like Douglass would not easily fit into Rawls's social union of social unions. A society where all men are guaranteed an equality of esteem must be one in which each man's self-esteem *is* entirely derivative from the way that all others regard him.

Rawls does indeed purport to acknowledge the superiority of men whose conduct is guided by internal standards of judgment to those who merely conform to the praise and blame of others. He presents as the highest stage of moral development the condition in which a person, having previously been led to act justly by his concern for other men's approbation, becomes attached to the principles of justice themselves, and conforms to them simply because "he now wishes to be a just person" (473). Such a person achieves what Rawls calls self-command (478). But this is a misnomer. The highest stage of moral development as Rawls conceives of it does not involve any independent reflection regarding how one should live, but simply embodies the deepest internalization of moral principles inculcated by society, principles which—in the ideal case—would conform to those laid down by Rawls. Self-command as Rawls understands it is equivalent to liberation as conceived of in Marxism: one "freely" commands himself to think and act as his Rawlsian or Marxian social environment has formed him to do.[18]

Rawls fails to recognize the contradiction between his praise of self-command and his contention that self-esteem is inevitably the product of social determination. To the extent that a man's sense of worth is dependent on what others think of him, he is not genuinely free. And on the other hand, to the extent that he is free, the possibility arises that he will disagree with the morality that society seeks to impose on him.

Rawls's understanding of self-respect is flawed because he underestimates and, in fact, denies the tension between the well being of the individual and that of society. For the sake of insuring that equality of esteem to which he thinks justice entitles all men, Rawls is prepared to sacrifice the very idea of individual merit or worth. To insist that the activities of the grass counter must be esteemed equally with those of Plato is to undermine the ground for esteeming any human activity, and hence for truly respecting others or oneself. Such a morality, precisely because it denies the ground of human dignity from which all rights must derive, thereby tends ultimately to undermine the foundation of justice. As Nietzsche foresaw, by depriving life of serious purpose, the morality of the last man generates nihilism. Rawls's Aristotelian Principle, which equates men's greatest achievements with "the spontaneous play of children and animals" (429), embodies this same nihilism. If adult life is reducible to play, why should human adults be entitled to any more rights than those we accord to children and animals? If the principles of justice themselves are analogous to those of a fair game (304), why should one choose to play this game rather than some other—say, the "games" of tyranny or murder?

In view of the radical deficiency of Rawls's understanding of the nature of human selfhood, and of the conditions of self-respect, his claim that a man who disregarded the demands of community as Rawls interprets them would be disfiguring himself is entirely unpersuasive. Let us grant Rawls's assertion that a man who never acted justly would deprive himself of the benefits of "friendship, affection, and mutual trust." The fact remains that Rawls has not demonstrated that his own particular account of justice is valid and hence that failing to conform to *it* would undermine friendship and trust. Moreover, to state the issue as one of *never* acting justly is a great oversimplification. The real problem of justice in this regard arises out of the difficulty of demonstrating the superiority of the claims of the *political* community to those of more particular groups such as one's family, friends, or even a mob of gangsters. The phenomenon of honor among thieves is well known; so also is the mobster who is quite capable of feeling indignation against "crime in the streets" in his own neighborhood. In order to demonstrate that the mobster's unjust way of life is truly detrimental to his own well being, Rawls would have to consider seriously the issue of what is good for man *by nature,* and show that justice is conducive to or at least not incompatible with that good. But by defining justice "without invoking a prior standard of human excellence" (327) and then providing no more than a formal and abstract demonstration of the goodness of being just in his sense, Rawls has foreclosed this possibility.

Just as Rawls's purported demonstration of the congruence of his account of justice with the human good fails, so too does his broader claim regarding the "stability" of the two principles. In addition to arguing that his conception of justice is conducive to the goods of self-respect and social union, Rawls tries to demonstrate the stability of this conception by contending that the reconstitution of society in accordance with its dictates would itself cause individuals to act more justly towards one another than they presently do. Thus the presumably peaceful revolution Rawls advocates would ultimately result in a greater degree of social stability. The central assumption underlying this argument is that the strength of a person's disposition to act justly is directly determined by the justness of the society or social group to which he belongs (473–74). In other words, the main reason why individuals act unjustly at present is that *society,* through its unjust distribution of primary goods, sets them a bad example. Hence one need only right that distribution, in accordance with Rawls's two principles, in order to transform men's conduct for the better (570).

What this wholly unsupported claim demonstrates is that Rawls has devoted no more serious thought to injustice than he has to justice. Rawls unhesitatingly assumes that practically all men will agree with his contention that justice is the greatest of human goods. Even if such agreement is not immediately forthcoming, he promises the reader that it will be, "once [men have] had full knowledge and experience" of a "perfectly just society" (477). In other words, once men have received what justice-according-to-Rawls dictates as their fair share, they should not want more. Hence they will not.

The foregoing argument disregards the possibility that there are goods more choiceworthy than justice to men, and that the major motivation of many who demand justice for themselves is not justice, but the primary goods to which they think justice entitles them.[19] Without admitting that it is even open to question, Rawls simply assumes the most extreme form of the conventional wisdom of liberal criminology, according to which most crime is the product of socioeconomic deprivation. And as for crimes which are not explicable in this manner, they are attributable to such perverted motives as a "love of injustice" (439), which, presumably, will wither away once Rawls's idea of social union is actualized.

Rawls cannot provide an adequate account of the causes of injustice because he refuses to acknowledge the essentially problematic character of justice itself. Leaving aside the already noted contradiction between Rawls's claim regarding the good of justice and the contractuarian foundation of his account of justice, Rawls's argument ignores the possibility that greater goods exist than those that are served either by justice or injustice. Entirely alien to Rawls's understanding is Aristotle's description of the good man as the most truly selfish of human beings, since such a man pursues the things that are truly good for himself. For Rawls, selfishness is simply an evil—because his theory of primary goods presupposes the perspective that Aristotle attributes to the vulgar, according to which the things that are good for the individual are objects like wealth, social status, and political power.[20] By denying the supreme goodness of contemplation as an end in itself (418), Rawls renders unbridgeable the gap between the selfish good of the individual and justice in at least the negative sense of abstention from injuring others.

In examining Rawls's specific prescriptions for just institutions in chapter 3 of the present volume, I observed that these prescriptions are far more conservative and less levelling than the character of Rawls's argument for his principles in part 1 would have led one to believe. Nonetheless, Rawls's relatively innocuous, if confused, prescriptions for political economy are occasionally interrupted, as I noted, by vituperative denunciations of the injustice of existing liberal polities. The account of the good in part 3 of *A Theory of Justice* reveals the spirit that underlies those denunciations, as well as some of Rawls's suggestions in part 1 (which he fails to elaborate in part 2) for particular methods of redressing nature's "injustice." It is a spirit that I believe is fundamentally antithetical not only to liberalism but to liberty. Herein lies the truly dangerous aspect of *A Theory of Justice*. Rawls adheres to and advocates an attitude of simple hostility to the principle that some men, gifted with superior abilities or possessed of unusual industry, should enjoy the fruits of their labors (including some degree of public admiration and honor), without making amends to others for their ability or achievement. Were a government to attempt to carry out the general spirit of Rawls's conception of justice, as opposed to the scheme of institutions actually proposed in part 2, it would become quite difficult to say just which class of men is truly least advantaged, for it seems that the greatest misfortune one can suffer in Rawls's well-ordered society (576) is to be born with a superior nature! Even though he acknowledges that "it is natural to experience a loss of self-esteem . . . when we must accept a lesser prospect of life for the sake of others" (181), Rawls infers from this fact not that superior individuals should enjoy opportunities that accord with their capacities, but rather that their achievements should be *held down* unless they can be shown to serve the well being of the least advantaged. For the sake of guaranteeing that all men, regardless of their natural inequalities, may "equally . . . further their aims" (97), Rawls is prepared to redress such inequalities by such means as spending more "on the education of the less rather than the more intelligent" (100–101).[21] And he goes so far as to suggest (fortunately without carrying it further) the possibility of adopting "eugenic policies, more or less explicit," as an additional means to the equalization of mankind (107).

Since even Rawls's difference principle would still allow unlimited inequalities of wealth to exist, there is no reason to assume that it would mitigate the loss of self-esteem that he alleges is caused by such inequalities. As we saw in chapter 3, nothing in the difference principle itself—as opposed to the particular consequences Rawls arbitrarily claims to infer from it—would require any alteration whatsoever in the present structure of Western liberal societies. Thus if it were true that inequality is incompatible with self-esteem on the part of the less advantaged, Rawls's arguments would hold equally against his own well-ordered society.

But there is no reason to accept the premise that happiness and self-esteem for the generality of men are incompatible with an inequality of wealth, position, and public honor. Most men who practice a trade or profession with a reasonable degree of success, earn a wage adequate to meet their basic material needs, and enjoy the blessings of family and friends, manage, so it would seem, to be fairly contented with themselves without spending too much time worrying over the existence of some men wealthier or more famous than themselves. (As Irving Kristol has observed, "the American working class . . . are far less consumed with egalitarian bitterness or envy than are college professors or affluent journalists.")[22] The political and economic conditions for such happiness are more prevalent in the United States and other Western liberal democracies today than in any other regimes in history. And the success and prosperity of these countries derive in no small measure from their allowing men to earn an inequality of wealth, and consequently of societal esteem, in accordance with their talents and efforts.

As Kant taught, and as the example of contemporary liberal democracies demonstrates, there is no inconsistency between allowing inequalities in wealth and achieved position to persist and at the same time treating all men with a certain basic respect and decency, simply in view of their humanity. The political structure of liberal society as it exists, for instance in the United States, works precisely to secure to *all* men an equality in those fundamental rights to which they are entitled. But one of those fundamental rights, as specified in the Declaration of Independence, is to the pursuit of happiness, i.e., to pursue one's own well being rather than being enslaved to the whims and unjustified demands of others.

Contrary to his claim (319), Rawls's account of justice is certainly not the expression of a democratic ethos, at least as that ethos has traditionally been understood in America.[23] The foremost theorists and statesmen of American democracy—such men as Jefferson, Madison, and Lincoln—were concerned to promote and reward the development of individual talents. Their principles could not be more remote from Rawls's doctrine, according to which differences in men's intelligence, industry, character, and even their sense of justice are unearned and hence (at least in the case of the first two) require redress (73-74, 83-84, 110-14, 310-12, 506). Rawls's denial that his conception of justice originates in feelings of envy and resentment (540-41) is unpersuasive. This conception expresses precisely that harmful form of the passion for equality that one of democracy's greatest and most thoughtful friends, Alexis de Tocqueville, most feared: the desire to pull others down to one's level rather than striving to demonstrate one's own ability and hence earn others' respect through achievement.[24] Rawls's interpretation of justice accords perfectly with Thrasymachus's view of the just man as an unfortunate dupe who serves others' well being at the expense of his own.[25] One cannot escape the conclusion, therefore, that *A Theory of Justice* is a parody of justice.

5

MORAL THEORY VERSUS POLITICAL PHILOSOPHY

> *The laws of conscience, which we say are born of nature, are born of custom; each man, holding in inward veneration the opinions and the morals approved and accepted around him, cannot break himself loose from them without remorse, or apply himself to them without self-satisfaction.*
>
> Montaigne
>
> *Surely, virtue is not the ruin of those who possess her, nor is justice destructive of a city.*
>
> Aristotle, *Politics*

1

In the preceding chapters I have tried to demonstrate both that the method by which Rawls purports to derive his two principles of justice is unsound, and that the principles themselves constitute a radically defective account of justice. My intention in this concluding portion of my analysis will be to trace these particular deficiencies of Rawls's methodology and doctrine to what I believe is their underlying cause: the defectiveness of his conception of political philosophy as such. I hope to demonstrate not only that a science of moral theory as Rawls conceives it is a poor substitute for political philosophy as the latter enterprise has traditionally been understood, but that such a science is inherently incapable of saying anything either meaningful or serious about moral or political issues. Since—as numerous studies of *A Theory of Justice* in journals of philosophy make evident—Rawls's understanding of political philosophy is one that is widely shared in certain fundamental respects by his colleagues, my criticisms are intended to have relevance to a broad trend in contemporary Anglo-American philosophy.

I began my analysis in chapter 1 by alluding to the peculiarity of the manner in which Rawls—by contrast, for instance, with Plato and Aristotle—conceives of his enterprise. Whereas political philosophers traditionally endeavored to describe the *nature* of justice, Rawls's express purpose both in *A Theory of Justice* and in his other writings has been to devise a theory that would account for or explicate men's *judgments* of justice. Rawls's endeavor rests, as was noted in chapter 1, on a presupposition about the adequacy of men's sense of justice that embodies serious epistemological difficulties which the author never resolves.

Rawls's peculiar conception of his enterprise severely constricts its scope as compared with the philosophic tradition. In particular, it results in a severance of the study of moral issues, with which Rawls is concerned, from the study of political and social *fact*. Rawls believes it is possible to elucidate the meaning of justice simply by alluding to what he believes are men's considered judgments about the subject, without having to formulate that conception in the light of an empirical examination either of the particular practical issues that give rise to the problem of justice, or of the problems involved in actualizing a conception of justice. As we have seen, Rawls postpones the elaboration of the practical political consequences of his theory of justice, and his purported (but purely formal) demonstration of its stability, until after the principles themselves have been laid down. And throughout the book Rawls expressly omits to consider fundamental practical issues, either arbitrarily assuming a particular psychological or sociological law to fit his requirements, or else leaving a problem aside to be considered by exponents of the various social sciences. Underlying this procedure is a specific understanding of the relation of moral theory to the social sciences which Rawls explains as follows:

> . . . while the theory of price, say, tries to account for the movements of the market by assumptions about the actual tendencies at work, the philosophically favored interpretation of the initial situation [the original position from which the principles of justice were derived] incorporates conditions which it is thought reasonable to impose on the choice of principles. By contrast with social theory, the aim is to characterize this situation so that the principles that would be chosen, whatever they turn out to be, are acceptable from a moral point of view. [120]

In sum, moral theory has nothing to say about, and no need to investigate independently, "the actual tendencies at work" in political life. Herein, as I have suggested previously, lies the secret of a great deal of the appeal that Rawls's book has had for contemporary social scientists. His conception of political philosophy as moral theory served to meet a widely felt need on the part of social scientists who were troubled by attacks on their disciplines in recent years for being value-free and hence irrelevant to the fundamental political and social problems facing the world.[1]

Many social scientists who were caught up in the wave of political passion that swept through the academy shortly before Rawls's book was published felt a conflict between the value-free presuppositions underlying their work and their desire to express and advance particular political commitments. Rawls's book seemed to arrive at just the right time to offer a way out of this dilemma. With little exaggeration, one can say that Rawls's conception of political philosophy is the mirror image of modern, positivistic social science: whereas the latter aspires to be value-free, the former is fact-free.

By placing the sanction of philosophy behind the tenets of contemporary academic liberalism, Rawls warmed the hearts of many fellow academicians who share his political preferences. But the special appeal of *A Theory of Justice* for social scientists in particular lay in its specific conception of the relation between political philosophy and social science. Rawls proved that he was not one of those uncooperative philosophers who raise impolite questions about the presuppositions of contemporary social science: e.g., its assumptions that human things can be studied in a value-free manner, and that they conform to hidden laws having the same regularity as those that govern the physical universe. Quite the contrary: Rawls not only presupposes the validity of contemporary social science, he seems to demonstrate that such a discipline is essential to the advancement of justice.

Rawls proposes what sounds like a neat division of labor between the philosopher and the social scientist: the philosopher determines what justice is, while the social scientist shows him how to bring it about. Thus the conscience of the value-free political scientist, economist, or sociologist regarding the worth of his work is salved. No further inquiry on his own part into troubling ethical issues is required. He can safely return to the conduct of his research, confident in the knowledge that, however dry or trivial it may seem, it will ultimately serve to promote the cause of justice as described by Rawls. And in the evening this same social scientist can dash off a letter to the editor or even join a demonstration himself, knowing that his political commitments have been given the status of principles of justice by a distinguished philosophical scholar.

Regrettably for the social scientist's peace of mind, I do not believe that this purported resolution of his dilemma is valid. On the contrary, moral theory as exemplified by *A Theory of Justice* simply represents the obverse side of the grievous harm that the study of human phenomena suffered when men undertook to sever the study of political facts from that of values. When social science declared its independence from political philosophy, the effect was not only to deprive the former of serious content, but also to forsake the noble title of the latter to an abstract logic of arbitrary personal preferences that is undeserving of such a title. If political philosophy in the proper sense—and hence, an adequate social science—is to be restored, it is necessary for us to be quite clear on how the former differs from moral theory as conceived by Rawls.

As the ablest critics of contemporary social science have demonstrated, it is simply not possible to separate facts from values in the study of human things, since the most interesting and important human things are inherently and necessarily the objects of praise and/or blame.[2] The attempt to exorcise issues of value from social science inevitably results either in the concentration on abstractions and trivialities or else in the surreptitious inclusion of evaluative premises that are never subjected to rational questioning. Thus it was rightly said of the practitioners of behavioral political science that they unknowingly emulate Nero in fiddling while Rome burns.[3] But the consequences of the unrighteous indignation and barren doctrinairism that Rawls's moral theory promotes may be more directly harmful than that. I believe it is fair to say that Rawls unknowingly helps to light the match that would burn Rome down. His direct contribution to that conflagration is, one must admit, infinitesimally small. But the more seriously troublesome harm of *A Theory of Justice* lies in its power of example: i.e., as an example of how the queen of the sciences may be corrupted into an ideology that serves to promote the dominant prejudices of the day rather than to question them.

In order to substantiate these charges, let me begin by reconsidering the original problem that gave rise to Rawls's project in the first place: the failure of existing moral theories to conform to the considered judgments issuing from men's sense of justice. The consequences of utilitarianism, in particular, as Rawls sketched them, appeared to be pernicious indeed: radical inequality, slavery, even (one might imagine) the persecution of an innocent man would be justified by the utilitarian if they promoted the "average utility" or the "net balance of satisfaction" in a society. That no major utilitarian thinker actually believed that such practices were in fact ordained by his principle is, according to Rawls, beside the point: what is critical is that utilitarianism in principle allows such practices to be defended. Hence the need, according to Rawls, for a new moral theory that, by establishing the priority of justness to good-ness, would put men's fundamental rights safely beyond the power of the principle of utility (or that of perfection) to undermine them.

The essential problem with this argument is, I believe, that it radically misrepresents the problem of justice. Each of the various moral theories, as Rawls constructs them, suffers from the fundamental defects of abstractness and irrelevance to reality. These theories each conceive of men in a wholly unreal way—as isolated receptacles among whom different quantities of unspecified satisfactions are to be distributed. But it is altogether impossible to determine what a just distribution of goods would be unless one knows *what* things are good for men, given their natures; what the relative value of the different good things is; how much of them is available; how far different goods are compatible with one another; and how far it is possible for government to influence their distribution. There are no such things as satisfactions that are qualitatively different but quantitatively commensurable, just as there are no such beings as persons who "have moral convictions" but "do not know what these convictions are" (220). Because there is no conceivable human situation that could resemble Rawls's original position, the debate over which set of principles would be accepted in such a situation has no possible relevance to human affairs.

In objecting to utilitarianism, on the ground that it unjustly demands that some men sacrifice their own well being merely so that the average utility or net balance of satisfaction in their society can be increased, Rawls never shows that any actual political society acted or attempted to act on such a principle. There is a good reason for this: the proposal of such a sacrifice is not one to which any sane man would be likely to agree in practice, and consequently it is not one to which any advocate of some particular policy would appeal if he hoped to influence other men.[4]

Each of the moral theories Rawls constructs, including his own, dis-regards the essentially political character of the human condition. All human beings live in political societies, and there is a reciprocal relation between the well being of a political community as such and the welfare of the human beings who compose it. On the one hand, no political society can survive unless the government provides the citizenry with adequate positive as well as negative incentives to obey and support it. On the other hand, the well being of every individual is fundamentally dependent on the survival and well being of the political community to which he belongs.[5]

Given the human condition, the way in which fundamental questions of justice actually arise is not in the form of disputes over whether the satisfaction of a given class or individual is to be promoted per se. Rather, because of the connection between each individual's well being and that of the political community as a whole, sacrifices of a person's private interests are demanded on behalf of the common good of the community, upon which his good in a more fundamental way depends. Even when policies are proposed that would seem clearly to benefit some classes at the expense of others' short-range interests—antipoverty legislation, for instance—these policies are justified by their advocates in the public forum on the ground, not that some theory requires that Peter be deprived to satisfy Paul, but that the community as a whole will benefit from them (in this case, presumably, because the loyalty of the poor to their country will be promoted, crime may be reduced, everyone's feeling of security against poverty will be increased, the nation's world prestige will gain, etc.). This holds, not only for legislation which favors the less advantaged, but also for institutions that give special privileges to the upper classes. Thus Burke and Hegel, as Rawls acknowledges, contended that political society requires a hereditary, aristocratic class if it is to be well governed, and consequently "that the whole of society including the least favored benefit from certain restrictions on equality of opportunity" that make such an aristocracy possible (300–301).

Because Rawls refuses to consider the kind of practical issues with which Burke and Hegel dealt while he is formulating his two principles, he can make it seem, for the moment, as if those principles promise to advance the popular causes of equality and liberty more than other philosophers' teachings do. But the abstractness of Rawls's principles and their lack of any empirical foundation make this appearance a spurious one. Consider, for instance, Rawls's case against John Stuart Mill. Rawls finds Mill's arguments on behalf of liberty, "cogent as they are," to be unsatisfactory because "they . . . will not, it seems, justify an equal liberty for all" (210). That is, while Mill himself favored the principle of equal liberty, at least in civilized societies where the conditions for its actualization are met, his arguments in favor of liberty rest on empirical considerations. By deriving the case for liberty from what would serve human ends, Mill left open the possibility, at least in principle, that those ends would under some circumstances best be promoted by limiting the liberty of some men more than that of others (210–11). By contrast, Rawls claims, his own theory of "justice as fairness provides . . . strong arguments for an equal liberty of conscience" and for the other "equal liberties" (211). But what arguments are these? Merely the circular contention that equal liberty accords with Rawls's sense of justice—*regardless* of its political consequences! The alleged superiority of Rawls's deontological theory to Mill's "teleological" one lies simply in Rawls's refusal to consider, in devising his principles, whether their consequences would actually be beneficial to men. Because Mill's argument for liberty rests on "precarious calculations" and "controversial and uncertain premises" (211), Rawls's alternative approach is simply to *assert* that justice requires equal liberty and not allow any controversy about it.

Rawls's rejection of Aristotle's political teaching rests on no firmer a foundation than does his critique of Mill. In viewing the problem of justice as one of distributing quantities of satisfactions without regard to qualitative differences among them, and in viewing the good of society as merely a sum of individual utilities, Rawls indicates (as more than one commentator has observed)[6] that, despite his criticisms of utilitarianism, he fundamentally accepts the Benthamite perspective. Because he is unable to see beyond that perspective, his purported refutation of the Aristotelian view "directing society to arrange institutions and to define the duties and obligations of citizens so as to maximize the achievement of human excellence" (325) is based on a fundamental misreading of Aristotle. Rawls treats what he labels the "principle of perfection" as if, in a manner akin to his own theory or to his version of utilitarianism, it simply demanded the sacrifice of some men's well being for the sake of promoting that of others (330). Perfectionism as Rawls presents it is an unrealistic doctrine for the same reason that the other theories he describes are: it views men as isolated individuals and commands that some men sacrifice simply so that others can gain. But this is not Aristotle's view. One cannot appreciate Aristotle's argument without viewing the claims of virtue in the light of their effect on the common good, as he did.[7] And, understood in that way, Aristotle's teaching is deserving of a much more serious consideration than Rawls gives it.

Rawls is simply oblivious to the kinds of substantive issues raised by Aristotle, Burke, Hegel, and Mill. This very dismissal of objections to the reigning egalitarian orthodoxy, however, seems to lie at the root of much of his book's appeal to readers who are anxious to have their political commitments given a theoretical justification. Thus so long as Rawls avoids considering political *realities*, it may indeed appear that he has set forth "the sort of solid theoretical underpinning that social democrats . . . have needed to ground their views of social justice."[8] It is easy enough for Rawls to score points with less thoughtful readers by telling them that he is in favor of everyone's pursuing his own conception of the good, without admitting that genuinely different conceptions of the good are incompatible with one another and would require conflicting conditions for their realization. It is similarly easy for him to favor both an equality of political influence for all and the securing of men's rights even against the majority will, without considering the extent to which these two objects are compatible: he need only disappear offstage with the remark that "I do not wish to pursue these matters further" (231), or leave the question to be resolved by political sociology (226-27). In promising men everything they desire without considering whether and how these things may be attained, Rawls emulates the politician who favors increases in public spending for every conceivable purpose but absents himself from any discussion of how tax revenues are to be raised to pay for them.

It is Rawls's fervent hope "to postpone the day of reckoning as long as possible" and to "try to arrange society so that it never comes" (303). However, as anyone who ever borrowed from a loan shark (but, unfortunately, too few politicians) could have told Rawls, that day comes quite soon. Once Rawls begins to treat the application of his theory to political life, he is forced to *retract* the substantive claims he had made in his purported refutation of other theories. Thus he admits that Mill may have been correct in opposing an equal political liberty for all men (232-33). Nor does he make any attempt to refute the arguments of Burke and Hegel on behalf of aristocracy. Rawls himself recommends that the principle of equal liberty be maintained only under certain special (but ill-defined) conditions (152). And he concedes in a footnote that even a feudal system might be compatible with the two principles (74n.). Some liberalism![9]

The only qualification Rawls adds to Burke's and Hegel's arguments in behalf of an inequality of liberty and privilege is that in addition to showing that it benefits "the whole of society including the least favored," the advocate of inequality "must also claim that the attempt to eliminate these inequalities would so interfere with the social system and the operations of the economy that in the long run anyway the opportunities of the disadvantaged would be even more limited" (301). But this qualification is a meaningless one, and adds nothing to what Burke and Hegel said. It presupposes an isolation of the good of the least favored from that of the whole of society that, as I have noted, does not correspond to the realities of political life. No one's life, liberty, or property—to say nothing of nobler goods—would have any security in a society that was *not* well governed, or to which the loyalty of *all* classes was not maintained. It is for this reason that the question of how a particular class deserves to be treated cannot be settled except in light of a determination of the good of the whole of society. Even if it were not unjust arbitrarily to single out one class, such as the disadvantaged, for special treatment (as Rawls does), without regard to the effect that such treatment would have on the whole of society but merely because one's ethos commands it (319), to do so would not even be beneficial to that class. If one sought to expand "the opportunities of the disadvantaged" by policies that harmed the whole of society by alienating other classes or causing the quality of government to deteriorate, one would in the long run, but more fundamentally, be harming the disadvantaged as well.

2

In founding his account of justice on the dictates of his sense of justice and without any serious, empirical consideration of political life, and then attempting to impose the consequences of his two principles on political society, Rawls has stood political philosophy on its head. Underlying this approach is a radical misunderstanding of the nature of philosophy that derives from Rawls's unwarranted assumptions about the epistemological adequacy of his sense of justice. In order to get at the root of what is wrong with Rawls's conception of political philosophy, we must return to this problem.

As I noted in chapter 2, Rawls claims that his approach is distinct from the doctrine of intuitionism. But this claim is a misleading one, founded on the rather peculiar definition Rawls gives of intuitionism. As another philosophical scholar, R. M. Hare, observes, "Rawls does not call himself an intuitionist; but he certainly is one in the usual sense."[10] As his frequent[11] references to his sense of justice or intuition indicate, Rawls agrees with what is normally understood as the essential principle of intuitionism: the doctrine that the truths of morality must ultimately be derived from intuition rather than from reason or nature. Rawls's only disagreement with intuitionism as he describes it concerns the question of whether moral judgments must be based on a "plurality of first principles" that are known and applied intuitively in particular cases, or whether men's moral intuitions can be organized around a more limited number of principles that are applied in accordance with fixed priority rules (such as the priority of liberty [34]). I suggest, however (as Hare also seems to), that this issue is of little significance in the end. Sooner or later, Rawls agrees with the intuitionists, moral beliefs and principles must be traced to intuitions, than which there can be no higher authority. Neither for Rawls nor for the other intuitionists is it the function of philosophy to *question* men's intuitions; rather, the philosopher can do nothing more than elucidate their implications.

The fundamental reason for Rawls's criticism of intuitionism as he defines it is a practical rather than an epistemological one. As he indicates in a passage quoted in chapter 2, Rawls fears that intuitionism, by failing to specify how weights should be assigned to competing principles of justice, will undermine the means for bringing about an agreement among men regarding justice. The alleged superiority of Rawls's theory to the intuitionist doctrine depends purely on Rawls's *hope* that the generality of mankind will find his principles intuitively appealing (48), and consequently will agree to use these principles to determine what justice requires in specific cases, rather than referring in each case to their particular (and presumably more variable) intuitions.

The importance Rawls attributes to securing men's agreement about the principles of justice causes him, I believe, to pay insufficient attention to seeking out the *truth* about justice. Rawls's fundamental motivation, in sum, is ideological in the literal sense, rather than genuinely philosophical.[12] He practically admits as much by indicating at numerous points that he has passed over difficulties in his conception of justice so as to give it the simplicity necessary for it to be universally adopted (14, 142, 510, 517, 585). For Rawls social wisdom dictates "the need for clear and simple principles"; hence for instance, in defining rationality, he strives "to avoid introducing into it any controversial ethical elements" (14, 90). Astonishingly, Rawls seems to believe that fundamental ethical controversies can be eliminated from political life by the simple device of accepting principles that ignore those controversies.

That Rawls himself is unaware of how moral theory as he pursues it differs from political philosophy in the traditional sense is indicated by the fact that he cites the procedures of both Socrates and Aristotle as a precedent (49, 51n.). The deficiencies of moral theory can most easily be brought out, however, by contrasting Rawls's approach with that of each of these philosophers.

As was noted in chapter 1, Rawls calls his procedure Socratic because it entails comparing a tentative theory of justice with the considered judgments that men already make without that theory, and then gradually altering either the theory, the judgments, or both until a fit is achieved between the two (49). Rawls thinks that through such a process he is emulating the Socratic dialectic. But this seeming similarity conceals a radical difference between the two approaches concerning the *source* of the changes that may occur in men's principles or their judgments as the result of engaging in dialectic. For Socrates such changes are the product of reason, which, by demonstrating a contradiction either within a particular opinion or among a set of seemingly plausible opinions, demonstrates the need to transcend the previous opinion(s) by pursuing a sounder understanding that will eliminate the contradiction. For Rawls, on the other hand, a person's decision to alter his previous moral opinions upon being confronted with a new set of principles comes about simply as the consequence of his finding the principles to constitute "an intuitively appealing account of his sense of justice" (48). In other words, the alteration of a person's moral opinions that occurs through the process of moral theorizing is not one that ultimately results from reason. Moral theory is the slave of intuition.

Rawlsian moral theory resembles Socratic dialectic in that each aspires to end in an agreement among the participants to a discussion. But here a further difference needs to be pointed out. The *philosophic* goal of Socratic dialectic (as distinguished from its rhetorical, defensive one) is to achieve an agreement that is based on mutual recognition of the truth. Rawls, on the other hand, who refuses to attribute objective value to having true beliefs rather than false ones (419), makes no mention of truth as the proper object of moral theory. For Rawls what counts is simply that men should be brought to agree on *some* notion of justice, one that conforms at the same time to their intuitions. It is this goal that gives Rawls's enterprise its essentially ideological character.

The different goals that Rawls and Socrates pursue through dialectic are reflected in the kinds of opinions about morality that each philosopher considers. Throughout the dialogues of Plato and Xenophon, the reader finds Socrates conversing with a practically unlimited variety of types of human beings holding beliefs about the good and the just that differ enormously (consider, for instance, the apparent gap between the views of justice set forth by Cephalus and Thrasymachus in book 1 of Plato's *Republic*). None of the opinions set forth by Socrates' various interlocutors may correspond to what Rawls would call a moral point of view—but they do represent the beliefs of actual human beings who are actively concerned to promote their respective well being as they perceive it. These are the beliefs with which the statesman—and any thinker who purports to give him genuine guidance about justice—must deal.

Whereas Socrates works out an account of justice by taking the various claims of actual human beings seriously, and determining the extent to which those claims may be reconciled with one another through a rational critique of the conception of the good implicit in each one, Rawls's procedure, as we have seen, is almost entirely the opposite. Beginning with the assumption that the fundamental dictates of his own sense of justice are correct, Rawls thinks that he can lead other men to agree to those dictates simply by dismissing all claims that conflict with them as of no value (261). Thus the agreement at which Rawls arrives is entirely an *artificial* one, having no reference to the actual claims and interests of humanity. Not only does Rawls limit his consideration of alternative views to other theories that have been deprived of substantive political content, he tests those theories only by examining whether they are more or less in accordance with his sense of justice than those of his own theory! It is as if the *Republic* had been written by Cephalus, who selected a cast of characters for the dialogue with a view, not to their representing the variety of actual political beliefs and claims, but rather to their either already agreeing with him or their being so pliable that they would assent to anything he said after he had pronounced it immoral to do otherwise.

Underlying the difference between the procedures employed by Rawls and Socrates is a substantive issue, of which Rawls seems quite unconscious, regarding the relation between human thought and reality. Both Rawls and Socrates pursue their investigations by means of the examination of human opinions. But for Socrates such examination is a means of access to the reality that is reflected, but at the same time partially obscured, in each of those opinions.[13] As he indicates through the beautiful metaphor of the cave in Plato's *Republic,* the common human situation is to see things only through the medium of opinions which have been inculcated by one's parents, the political authorities, and the poets.[14] It is the goal of philosophy, as Socrates conceives of it, to liberate the individual from the cave, by enabling him to work his way towards an understanding of things in their true being.

What is critically absent in Rawls's account of moral theory is any reference to an objective truth towards which men's varying opinions point and which it is the object of philosophy to discern. His denial of an authoritative role to reason is simply the obverse side of his disregard of nature. For Rawls men's intuitions about justice must be regarded as the ultimate standard of truth, because he denies that justice has any meaning going beyond what the generality of men in a society think about it. This fact is well brought out by Rawls's comparison of moral theory to scientific theory in his chapter 1. Although Rawls distinguishes between these two sorts of theory, as I noted earlier, on the ground that the former, unlike the latter, may result in an alteration of the phenomena it describes—the moral judgments that men make—he suggests that they are in other respects analogous. Just as the astronomer attempts to develop laws that account for the motions of the heavenly bodies, the moral theorist constructs principles that aim to describe men's moral judgments. What is striking about this analogy is that the perceived *facts* that the astronomer attempts to describe are being compared to the *judgments* that, in Rawls's view, correspond to the physical realities with which astronomy is concerned. The substance of justice is identical with the sum of the opinions men have *about* it. Hence, there exists no objective or natural standard against which those opinions or intuitions might be judged correct or incorrect.

I submit that Rawls's equation of justice with men's judgments about it is grossly at variance with our everyday understanding of what we are doing when we make such judgments. We are all aware that men's judgments of justice frequently disagree. But in debating whether a given act, law, man, or government is just or unjust, we presuppose that there does exist a standard of justice independent of what particular groups of men feel or think about it, a standard rooted in our perception of the nature of things. It is the existence of such a standard, dimly perceived by all of us, that enables us, despite our disagreements, to dispute about the precise meaning of justice in particular cases. The very fact that we speak of having an opinion *about* justice—just as we have opinions about the weather— implies a belief that there is such a thing as justice, independent of our opinions, which our opinions attempt to describe.

In order to see what is paradoxical in Rawls's conception of moral theory, one need only imagine how a comparable description of physical theory would run. To identify the subject matter of moral philosophy as men's judgments about the good and the just is analogous to identifying astronomy with the description of men's beliefs about the planets—a description in which Ptolemaic views would have to be given at least equal weight (by virtue of the number of men who adhered to them) as post-Copernican ones. As Hare observes, such a conception of science might have appealed to "medieval flat-earthers."[15] But, recent debates about the nature of scientific truth notwithstanding, I do not believe that any physical scientist would accept such an account of his endeavor.

It is manifest that there are important differences between the procedures of moral and political philosophy and those of natural science. Most prominent among them is the fact that the political philosopher deals with phenomena that have no *tangible* reality, and consequently can be grasped only by considering the human beliefs about them that are manifested in men's speeches. One cannot "see" a government, a law, or an obligation, as one can a star or a paramecium: their reality is visible only to the eye of the mind.[16] It is this fact that seems to have led Rawls to the conclusion that the meaning of justice is identical with the sum of the things that are commonly believed or said about it: because justice can be seen only *through* the mind, he presumes that it must be identical with the beliefs that are equally *present* in all men's minds. The most obvious difficulty with this presumption is the fact that moral and political matters are the subjects of such extreme disagreement among men that it is doubtful that any consistent principle of political justice could be stated that would readily win universal assent. In view of Rawls's aim of unifying men's beliefs about justice, therefore, it is not surprising that he shies away from giving serious consideration to substantive views of justice that differ from his own. Rawls perceives few of the objections that can be raised against his intuitions, it seems, because he doesn't want to see them: every dissenting view is a further obstacle in the way of the unanimity that he aims to secure.

Rawls's claim that his procedure is analogous to Aristotle's is no more valid than his assertion that it is Socratic. Aristotle, unlike Rawls, treats common opinion as a starting-point for philosophic analysis, rather than as the self-sufficient criterion of truth. Whereas Rawls seldom looks beyond the narrow range of moral judgments made by men who agree with him at the outset (and disposes of the contrary views in an abrupt manner), Aristotle considers the range of common opinion in its full diversity, and finds that men's common beliefs are mutually, as well as internally, contradictory on many points. Hence Aristotle is compelled to look behind those opinions to the reasons on which they are grounded, and to weigh those reasons in an essentially Socratic manner in order to extract the element of truth that they contain. When Aristotle proposes to consider the nature of the good in the light of the common opinions about it, on the ground that all the facts harmonize with the true view,[17] he does not mean that all men, when confronted with his account, would immediately agree with it. Given the diversity of views about happiness that he cites in the same chapter, and his later remarks about the impotence of speeches in influencing most men's conduct or fundamental beliefs,[18] Aristotle would deny that such agreement can be expected. The diversity of men's beliefs does not, however, make an objectively valid account of the good or the just unattainable. Most men, not being philosophic, devote little thought to the grounds on which their moral and political opinions rest. But the philosopher, by examining these grounds in an impartial manner, should be able to transcend the bias and shortsightedness that distort common opinion. To say that his account of the good and the just must harmonize with the common views means that the philosopher could defend his account by showing that it necessarily *follows from* each of the common views when the grounds of those opinions are uncovered.[19] Few men, indeed, have ever truly adhered to the conclusion Aristotle reaches in book 10 of the *Ethics* that the best and happiest way of life is that of philosophy; but the argument of the *Ethics* is aimed at showing how this conclusion utlimately derives from the premises embodied in the various common opinions.[20]

For Aristotle, then, the harmonization of opinions about morality can come about only as the consequence of the discovery of the truth concerning morality. Such a harmonization will be evident, moreover, only to the philosophic inquirer who engages in the rigorous process of reasoning necessary to separate out truth from falsehood in each opinion, and whose dedication to the pursuit of truth above all other goals frees him from the bias to which other men are prone.[21] The goals of truth and popular acceptance are not compatible; one must choose between them. Rawls, by positing an *actual* unanimity of opinion among men as the goal of moral theory, parts company with Aristotle on this fundamental issue. His explicit avoidance of controversial issues for the sake of making it more likely that his theory will be popularly accepted stands in the sharpest contrast to Aristotle's procedure.

3

Assuming that I have demonstrated the deficiencies of Rawlsian moral theory as a substitute for political philosophy in the traditional sense, it remains to consider what lent the underlying assumptions of this theory such plausibility as to appeal not only to Rawls but to so many of his commentators and critics. It is necessary in particular to reexamine the phenomenon that Rawls labels the sense of justice, which constitutes the very foundation of his theory.

Rawls's assumption that practically all normal, adult human beings possess a sense of justice that gives them adequate guidance regarding the just in most instances, and to some degree motivates them to act in accordance with its dictates, derives its greatest plausibility from the normal presumption or expectation of human law. In every political community the citizenry as a whole are expected to act in accordance with the dictates of justice, as embodied in the law. Regardless of whether ignorance of the law in some technical respect might occasionally excuse a particular crime, ignorance of justice is never an acceptable excuse, except as evidence of mental illness. The law presumes that knowledge of justice does not require any sophisticated sort of education, but is somehow learned by every man; and that this knowledge is accompanied by a capacity for acting in accordance with its dictates. Every citizen is expected to "know" not only *what* legal justice dictates, but that he *ought* to live in accordance with those dictates.

As is evident in his doctrine of civil disobedience, Rawls himself is far from equating the just with the legal. But—despite his account of moral education, which suggests the essentially cultural or social roots of the sense of justice—Rawls retains the law's notion that justice is relatively unproblematic, and can be adequately known by the individual if only he looks within himself. The variation in the conceptions of justice that characterize different societies seems in no way to have shaken Rawls's faith in the objectivity of each man's sense of justice, and hence in the possibility of establishing a theory of justice that all men can accept.

In viewing the sense of justice as an intuition, Rawls seems to have believed that he was conforming to the philosophic tradition, many of whose members have granted the need for some intuitive knowledge as the foundation of all reasoning. But the claim that men's knowledge of *justice* is intuitive is both more philosophically novel and more problematic than Rawls realizes. This fact can most easily be brought out by briefly recalling the classic treatment of philosophic intuition given by Aristotle.

Aristotle observes that all scientific or demonstrative knowledge is the product of reasoning, the premises of which "must be true, primary, immediate, [and] better known than and prior to the conclusion" of the syllogism. Since there cannot be infinite regress, the original premises from which all true reasoning and knowledge of the world are derived, such as the principle of contradiction and the sheer fact of the world's existence, must be known more directly and reliably than the conclusion of any syllogism. Aristotle's term for the faculty by which these ultimate premises are known is *nous*, "intuition" or "intellection."[22]

Nous plays a part, according to Aristotle, both in scientific knowledge and in the intellectual faculty concerned with matters of conduct, *phronesis*, "practical wisdom." But there is a critical difference between the two cases. It is in the case of scientific demonstration that *nous* supplies "the unchangeable and first terms" from which all subsequent reasoning proceeds. The role of *nous* in practical reasonings, on the other hand, is limited to supplying "the last and variable fact," "the ultimate particular" with which conduct is concerned, such as the recognition that the object of one's action is a human being.[23] Aristotle denies, in other words, that *nous* supplies any *practical* universals or intuitive rules of right to guide men's conduct.[24] In fact, even while asserting the existence of natural right, Aristotle denies the existence of any wholly invariable rules of justice: "while with us [human beings, as distinguished from the gods] there is something that is just even by nature, yet all of it is changeable." The first principles of human affairs are variable, because matters of practice or conduct depend on a variety of circumstances that are themselves changeable.[25] It is the task of the statesman, possessed of practical wisdom, to determine the means by which the good of the political community may be advanced in particular cases; evidently that goal may require modification even of the "natural" standards of right.

Whence the statesman's own knowledge of what constitutes the good of the community derives is not at first manifest in Aristotle's account. It is at least evident, however, that there is a considerable gap between this account of practical wisdom and the law's assumption that every individual knows what is just. Thus Rawls, by asserting the existence of moral intuitions that supply men with an adequate basis for right conduct, and even for questioning the law, has taken a major step beyond Aristotle's account of *nous*. In fact, if one were to except the particular eighteenth- and nineteenth-century tradition from which Rawls's approach ultimately derives, the only philosophic precedents for his assumption about moral intuition would seem to be Aquinas's doctrine of *synderesis,* the faculty that embodies the precepts of the natural law, and Kant's notion of an a priori moral law that is a necessary dictate of reason. But Aquinas's doctrine is dependent on a teaching of divine grace or revelation,[26] such as Rawls expressly denies presupposing (206, 217). And Rawls similarly disclaims the presupposition of a priori moral laws; his two principles are in any event essentially different in character from such laws.[27]

Given the novel character of his claims regarding moral intuition, one would surely have expected Rawls to provide an extensive argument justifying this claim. But he provides no such argument. Considering his own acknowledgment of the societal origins of men's sense of justice, it rather appears that Rawls has simply chosen to give a new label, and attach a greater sanctity, to the phenomenon that Socrates terms simply opinion (*doxa*). What for Socrates had been the starting-point of philosophic questioning is for Rawls its ultimate standard of truth.

It is an undoubted fact that all men *feel* on many occasions the kind of moral certainty to which Rawls alludes through his reference to the sense of justice. That there are some general precepts of justice on which all men, whatever their particular political beliefs, would be likely to agree—for instance, that an innocent person should not be punished for another man's crime—is powerful testimony that justice has, as Aristotle indicates, some natural and universal core. But such universal precepts are very far from the specific ordinances that Rawls claims to infer from his sense of justice. And his account of the sense of justice as a *motive* for action is, as I tried to show in chapter 4, wholly inadequate.

A far profounder analysis of what men call their conscience or sense of justice is provided by such political philosophers as Plato, Aristotle, and Montaigne. The phenomenon of conscience is ultimately rooted, these philosophers suggest, in men's susceptibility to praise and blame, or *amour-propre.* Every political society seeks to take advantage of this susceptibility by educating its members, from childhood, in the belief that conformity to the established laws and customs of that society is the most important, if not the only, criterion of human excellence.[28] Such education is particularly necessary because man is not by nature a lover of justice: were it not for his societally induced sense of shame—or, in the worst cases, his fear of punishment—each man would naturally seek to acquire as much as possible of what he understands to be the good things for himself, his family, and his friends, without regard to the well being or desert of other men.

Both because of the variety of regimes and hence of ruling classes, and also because of the variation in the circumstances in which particular political societies find themselves, different polities tend to embody different conceptions both of the good and of the just. The variety of regimes, and therefore of the corresponding spirit in which different groups of human beings are educated, is the root of the variation in the commonly accepted moral beliefs or seeming intuitions to which different peoples and groups adhere.[29] Those beliefs ultimately reflect not only the particular needs of a given society, but also the biases peculiar to that society's ruling class, be it one, few, or many; Christian or pagan; Lockean or Marxist.

Plato and Aristotle recognized that, given the relative weakness of reason (in force as well as in capacity) in most men, the maintenance of any decent civil society depends on the continued inculcation of a conventional morality that is accepted on the authority of parents, the city's rulers, the poets, and the generality of the citizen body. Most men's thought will be bound, and must be bound, by the moral opinions (and their theological support) that they were taught to believe as children. The "knowledge" that the law expects and demands of the citizenry concerning justice and morality is not a direct and rational apprehension of the truth, but a recollection of the undemonstrated *opinions* about right and wrong that were previously engraved on their minds. Hence Aristotle asserts that the starting-points of political and ethical science derive from a sound habitual upbringing: every well-brought-up human being knows that one ought to be just and obey the law.[30]

Even though the general acceptance of a conventional, habitual morality is the precondition of a civic order, however, it is neither identical, in truth, with the full form of human excellence and happiness, nor even a sufficient guide to the conduct of the city's affairs. To live as a merely moral man, never questioning the beliefs about justice that one was taught, is to remain among the inhabitants of Plato's cave, seeing only the shadows of images of the true things—seeing these things, in other words, only in the distorting mirror of common opinion.[31] It is the aim of philosophy to liberate from this situation those few men whose desire and capacity for knowledge enable them to experience such a liberation and at the same time guarantee against the abuse of their liberty. Philosophy teaches men to question all received opinions and intuitions, most particularly those that directly concern the issue of how one should live, in the light of reason. Such a pursuit, challenging (however circumspectly) men's most cherished and sacred beliefs, is always in tension with the political order. But it offers, at the same time, the best hope of making more tolerable the situation of those who remain in the cave, by introducing into the community's deliberations, when the city's leaders are "tame" enough to lend an ear, a somewhat greater degree of rationality.

Rawls, in setting out to promote a moral consensus founded on un-questioned intuitions, has sided with the city's prejudices, and against philosophy. This is not to say, however, that the version of justice he propounds would serve to strengthen the moral bonds that hold civil society together. There is always a danger, as we learn from Machiavelli, in a moral authority that exists in separation from political responsi-bility.[32] Enjoying as he does a position of academic eminence, in a society where the views of scholars and intellectuals are conceded almost the respect and veneration once accorded to those of churchmen, Rawls appears to be insufficiently cognizant of the risks of pronouncing an abstract morality that does not take account of the complexities of the statesman's task and of the limits of political possibility. In founding justice on intuition rather than on the consideration of reality, and in requiring that political institutions be "reformed or abolished" if they fail to conform to his pronouncements (3), Rawls has severed morality, not only from philosophy and religion, but also from prudence.

Himself a member of an intellectual class that is a prime beneficiary of a just and free regime, Rawls repays that regime with irresponsible denunciations and unreflective demands. It is for this reason that I think one may justifiably accuse Rawls's moral theory of exceeding the Neronian tendencies of previous deficient schools of philosophy and political science that have enjoyed popularity in this century.

4

The central intention of this study has been to demonstrate the defective-ness of *A Theory of Justice* as a purported work of political philosophy. I have attempted to trace the particular flaws in Rawls's arguments to the deficiency of his underlying conception of political philosophy as moral theory. A full account of the historical origins of Rawls's under-standing of political philosophy would be far beyond the scope of this work. In concluding my analysis, however, I would like to set forth some suggestions regarding that problem.

The character of the major alternatives to which Rawls compares his theory of justice—intuitionism and utilitarianism—indicates that Rawls is far from being the inventor of moral theory. Like Rawls's own theory, utilitarianism and intuitionism largely constitute attempts to explain the ground or source of men's conventional moral judgments, without ever questioning the substantive adequacy of those judgments.[33] Each of these doctrines has origins in British schools of philosophy that date from the nineteenth century. The non-substantive character of nineteenth-century British moral philosophy, presupposing rather than questioning the established morality, was pointed out by Friedrich Nietzsche, whose comment on the utilitarians could equally have been applied to most of their compatriots who thought of themselves as anti-utilitarian:

> Ultimately they all want *English* morality to be proved right—because this serves humanity best, or "the general utility," or "the happiness of the greatest number"—no, the happiness of *England*. With all their powers they want to prove to themselves that the striving for English happiness— I mean for comfort and fashion (and at best a seat in Parliament)—is at the same time also the right way to virtue; indeed that whatever virtue has existed in the world so far must have consisted in such striving.[34]

This older tradition of British moral philosophy has largely merged, under the influence above all of the Austrian expatriate Ludwig Wittgenstein, into the "ordinary language" or "conceptual analysis" approach that currently dominates philosophical scholarship in the English-speaking world. Rawls's own approach has certain obvious features in common with the ordinary-language movement. It is true that Rawls explicitly denies that his theory is intended "as a description of ordinary meanings," or in fact "that the notions of meaning and analyticity play [any] essential role in moral theory as I conceive of it" (xi, 10). But in previous articles that contained much of the fundamental thought elaborated in *A Theory of Justice,* Rawls described his work as "an analysis of the concept of justice."[35] Perhaps what led Rawls away from the terminology of conceptual or linguistic analysis was his recognition of the difficulty of showing that when men use the word "justice" they necessarily have anything like his two principles in mind.[36] The deeper agreement between Rawls and the practitioners of ordinary-language analysis, however, is in the denial that such terms as "goodness," "justice," or "virtue" can be said to have a meaning independent of what the generality of men of a given time or place intuit or say, respectively, about them. For Rawls it is the ordinary man's intuition or sense of justice that determines the reality of justice; for the ordinary-language philosopher it is the concepts of common discourse that constitute the limiting point of philosophic inquiry.[37] In neither case does philosophy have any substantive content, as it did for the great political philosophers of the tradition; rather than critically examining men's beliefs about justice, the moral theorist merely attempts to clarify the ordinances of men's intuitions or their grammar. For a long time, precisely because of its substantive barrenness, the approach to moral and political philosophy practiced by nineteenth- and twentieth-century British scholars had no direct political effect, for the morality they professed to explain was (as Nietzsche suggests) nothing other than the generally accepted principles of English gentlemanship and liberalism in which their regime was rooted.[38] We live at a time, however, when it is no longer fashionable for the intellectual or scholar to defer to the traditions that gave the England of a century ago its stability and civility. Instead, he is supposed to be above all a critic and a conscience to his society, demonstrating through his work a commitment to justice and social reform as the members of his class conceive of them. Thus the moral theorist is increasingly tempted to go beyond a merely abstract account of the source of men's moral judgments, and, under the guise of a description of the sense or concept of justice or morality, to express intuitive judgments requiring extensive changes in the political order.[39] Nothing in the premises of moral theory itself provides any ground for such judgments. Rather, having formerly derived his standard of morality from the established principles of his regime, the moral theorist now turns elsewhere—i.e., to whatever current social reform movement appeals to him—for his premises. Rawls, perhaps more than any of his colleagues, has succumbed to this temptation; and herein, I believe, lies the fundamental explanation of his book's popularity outside the philosophical "discipline."

A Theory of Justice represents, I have tried to suggest, the culmination of a decay in political philosophy that has been going on for more than a century. The essence of this decay is the severance of the study of morality from that of nature and ultimately, therefore, from politics. In order to understand the ultimate causes of this decay, one would have to look back to the public teachings of the great political philosophers of the sixteenth through eighteenth centuries who laid the foundations of modern liberalism. According to the view of nature set forth by Montaigne, Hobbes, and Locke, among others, the excellence of man has no foundation in nature, for nature is an all-encompassing machine composed of matter in motion that cannot be said to embody a purpose or, hence, a standard for judging man. The only purpose that can properly be attributed to man's nature is the pre-rational instinct he shares with the beasts to pursue his individual preservation. The awareness of the true character of nature, attained through philosophy, makes it possible (so these philosophers thought) to achieve a tremendous improvement in the human condition by reconstructing human thought in light of that awareness. Since morality and justice have no foundation in nature, they must be purely human constructs, originating in our minds. What our minds produce, we can reconstruct as we please. Since the one purpose that is fixed in man's nature is the instinct of self-preservation, morality should be reconstituted so as not to interfere with the maximal satisfaction of this instinct. Freeing men's minds from the superstition that attributes purpose or divine will to the world, so these philosophers argued, makes possible a political liberation from the tyranny and oppression that have been forced on humanity in the name of piety and virtue. Once it is understood that the only legitimate purpose of government is the security of men's life, liberty, and property, political life should become more stable and the contentment of the individual more secure.

The obfuscation of the fundamental political and moral issues, and the consequent withering away of political philosophy into moral theory, that have taken place in the English-speaking countries during the last two centuries, are ultimately due to the very success of the original modern project in these countries. It was the intention of the philosophic founders of liberalism to divert men from the most divisive moral, political, and religious questions,[40] both by encouraging a popular attitude of religious skepticism and by attracting them to the pursuit of unlimited material gain, newly liberated from moral and religious restraints. On the Continent, however, the depletion of nature by modern philosophy led subsequent thinkers, concerned to regain some standard of human excellence higher than that of the bourgeois, to replace nature with history as the foundation of such a standard. Thus liberalism was supplanted by the philosophy and ideology of history, culminating in the doctrine of historical relativism, the influence of which is still increasing.[41] In the English-speaking countries, on the other hand, the liberal teaching took such deep root and enjoyed such success that little reason was seen to question it until recently. Thus the denial that nature furnishes a standard for human excellence and morality led, not to a new political philosophy founded on a ground other than nature, but to the decay of Aristotle's architectonic science into the abstract analysis of the source within man's mind of the moral opinions upon which all decent men were supposed to agree.

The time when liberalism could be taken for granted is clearly over. If the liberal regime of constitutional democracy is worthy of being preserved (as I believe that any sober evaluation of the present alternatives to it will indicate), it can be defended only if men become conscious once again of its foundations—and of their controversiality. So long as political philosophy is identified with moral theory, it cannot provide us with such an awareness. As is evident in his dogmatic dismissal of political and moral views that differ from his own, Rawls's version of moral theory is in one sense a rather pathetic last-ditch effort on the part of liberalism to chase away the goblins of anti-liberal and relativist thought by pronouncing the incantation "immoral!" at them. Yet this defense carries within it, at the same time, the seeds of liberalism's own destruction. The anti-liberal impulse that underlies Rawls's liberalism is evident both in his dogmatic style of argument and in the tyrannical tendency that emerges most clearly in part 3 of *A Theory of Justice*. Even more ominous for liberalism are the implications of Rawls's theoretical assumptions— implications of which he seems quite unconscious. As Allan Bloom observes, Rawls's notion of a sovereign, value-creating self "had its origin in thinkers who were friends of neither reason nor liberalism," and is manifestly inconsistent with his professed liberalism.[42] Similarly, the historicist assumptions that underlie the ordinary-language school which in critical respects resemble Rawls's premises[43] point in a direction quite opposed to liberalism. And finally, there is Rawls's pitiful attempt to stretch the meaning of liberalism so wide that even Marxism can be accommodated within it.[44]

The widespread acclaim that *A Theory of Justice* has received from the academic community despite the book's manifold defects is on the one hand a disheartening sign of contemporary decay, not only in political philosophy, but in scholarship. But this acclaim can be taken at the same time as an indication of a growing dissatisfaction with positivistic social science and formalistic philosophy, and consequently of a renewed openness to genuinely philosophic reflection on the fundamental issues of morals and politics. What is needed, if the longing for such reflection is to receive its proper satisfaction, is a restored awareness of the nature of political philosophy in its proper sense, as that pursuit was understood by wise men from Plato to Nietzsche. A revival of the serious yet critical reading of the books that the great political philosophers have bequeathed to us will demonstrate, I believe, that these works still speak to our profoundest concerns in a way that is unmatched by any contemporary scribbling. If, by emphasizing the contrast between these books and *A Theory of Justice*, I have contributed in some small way to such a revival, then this study will have achieved its purpose.

EPILOGUE

The focus of this book has been on the particular arguments by which Rawls attempts to establish his account of justice, rather than on the more general societal ethos that *A Theory of Justice* embodies. In view of what I have tried to show are the radical deficiencies of Rawls's argument, however, the widespread acclaim that *A Theory of Justice* has received from the intellectual community seems explicable only in the light of something extrinsic to the quality of the author's reasoning: the fact that Rawls's sense of justice is widely shared by other members of the contemporary intellectual class in America. It seems appropriate to conclude this book, therefore, by commenting briefly on the sources of that influential ethos, and the reasons for its appeal.

The view of justice that is represented by Rawls's difference principle is expressive of what Charles Frankel has termed a "redemptive" egalitarianism.[1] Unlike the traditional liberal egalitariansim, this movement is not concerned with seeking to make inequalities of wealth, status, and power conform to inequalities of talent and effort. Its goal is rather to combat inequality *as such,* whether founded on convention or on nature, on industry or on luck.

One can find many examples of redemptive egalitarianism in contemporary American political thought and practice. It is expressed in attacks on the alleged injustice of inequalities of wealth and income—whether earned or not—both intra- and inter-nationally; in so-called affirmative action programs that require persons to be educated and hired according to racial and sexual quotas, without regard to the relative qualifications of non-"minority" groups; and in court-ordered school busing designed to overcome de facto racial segregation, so as to promote the goal of social homogeneity. What is remarkable about these movements is the social class in which they originate. Redemptive egalitarianism purports to elevate the condition of "oppressed" blue collar workers, racial minorities, former colonial peoples, and "unliberated" housewives. Yet its chief advocates come from one of the most privileged classes known to history—American intellectuals and professionals.

It would be comforting to accept the claim of the redemptive egalitarians that their demands are motivated by a selfless concern for the well being of others. Unfortunately, this claim is vitiated when one considers the particular character of the demands and the type of people who make them. The non-minority advocates of racial quotas in education and hiring are those who already enjoy secure and well-paid jobs themselves. They are quite ready to evince their concern for social justice by demanding that qualified white males step aside to increase the opportunities for those defined as minority groups—but never to give up their own jobs for this purpose. Similarly, they ardently demand that working class whites send their children to school with children from black slum areas—but seldom are willing to do so themselves. And the demand for income redistribution is made by professionals either wealthy enough to afford tax shelters that will shield them against most of the impact of higher taxation—or by intellectuals who *think* of themselves as having merely average incomes, ignoring certain important non-taxable benefits.[2]

The real root of the movement for redemptive egalitarianism is the phenomenon of liberal guilt—the feeling on the part of relatively wealthy and well-educated people that they must atone for their superior privileges by demonstrating their commitment to promote "social justice" for the less advantaged. This phenomenon is distinct from charity in the proper sense, precisely in the fact that it calls for no genuine sacrifice on the part of the would-be benefactor.[3] One could afford to overlook this fact if the *effect* of the egalitarian movement were to promote justice, whatever the motive that led to it. But this is not the case. Guilt, like its sister compassion, is a poor foundation for policy.[4] The person who is eager to assuage his guilt cares little about analyzing the real effects of a particular policy; it is sufficient that the proposed policy *seems* to benefit the "oppressed," and to call for sacrifices on the part of those others whom he believes to be unjustly privileged. The effects of the policies advocated by the redemptive egalitarians have been largely detrimental to the well being both of the United States as a whole and of the less advantaged in particular.[5]

Given its dubious results, the phenomenon of guilt about inequality calls for further scrutiny. As has frequently been remarked, the Western regimes in which this phenomenon has arisen are those in which not only society as a whole, but the lower class in particular, has achieved an unprecedented level of absolute material prosperity, and in which the principles of equality of opportunity (as opposed to hereditary class distinctions) and of equality before the law have been realized to an unparalleled degree. This success ought to be cause for congratulation rather than guilt. Why, then, is the fact of inequality, or so-called relative deprivation, suddenly the subject of so much concern?

The explanation of this concern has been provided by Tocqueville, and elaborated more recently by Irving Kristol. The radical social and economic mobility noted by Tocqueville in modern democracy undermined all hereditary distinctions of class. By making a man's wealth and status depend more on his own achievements than on those of his ancestors, this movement made society more just. But at the same time, it made *all* inequalities of wealth and status open to question. Because social and economic position were seen to fluctuate, they could no longer be accepted by men in general as the fixed dispensation of God or nature. A man's membership in the lower class seemed to imply some personal failing on his part, rather than being the result of fate. This feeling caused men to scrutinize more closely the merit of those who had achieved a superior status. Since most instances of great success embody some element of luck, it began to be doubted how far those in the upper class had really earned their position. This initial doubt ultimately inspired a more radical one: did *any* achievements entitle a man to enjoy more wealth and status than others possessed?

The great difficulty of the modern liberal economy, as Kristol has argued, is its inability to provide a *moral* justification for the distribution of income.[6] The advantage of the liberal economy, from the point of view of the common man, is that, by allowing men to earn rewards in proportion to their work, it gives them an incentive to contribute to the common stock of goods produced.[7] But however great the resultant increase in the general standard of living, inequalities that result from differential economic production lack the manifest legitimacy of older inequalities that were thought to be sanctioned by God or by differences in inherited virtue. Hence the effect noted by Tocqueville: the more equal that conditions become, the more outrageous the remaining inequalities are perceived, by some, to be.

Whatever may be the case in Europe, there is little evidence that the vast majority of Americans are fundamentally dissatisfied by the existence of inequality. As many commentators have observed, it is the sheer success

America has enjoyed in offering everyone an opportunity to better his condition that has protected this country against the kind of class conflict that European countries have undergone, and has consequently prevented the socialist movement from ever gaining much of a foothold here. Redemptive egalitarianism in this country is almost exclusively, as noted above, a movement of the intellectual class. It is this fact that gives rise to Kristol's highly persuasive explanation of the concerns underlying the egalitarian movement. That movement is rooted, Kristol argues, in the dissatisfaction of intellectuals with the bourgeois character of liberal society. The egalitarian argument of today is the direct heir, Kristol suggests, of the older, anti-egalitarian critique of commercial society, which scorned its money-mindedness and its lack of devotion to transcendent, self-sacrificing ideals. In sum, "The demand for greater equality has less to do with any specific inequities of bourgeois society than with the fact that bourgeois society is seen as itself inequitable because it is based on a deficient conception of the common good."[8]

If one were to pursue the implications of this line of thought seriously, one would be led to reconsider the liberal regime in the light of such alternatives as the aristocracy described by Tocqueville, or Rousseau's virtuous republic. But such reflections are seldom pursued by the new egalitarians. As exemplified by Rawls, they wish to have their cake and eat it, too—to enjoy the material prosperity and legal freedom that liberal society provides, while at the same time reaping the psychic rewards of self-satisfaction that result from their denunciations of the injustice of the liberal regime. If the effect of those denunciations is harmful, as I have argued, to the perpetuation of the liberal regime, the benefits of which these intellectuals wish to continue enjoying, then their stance is an irresponsible one.

Underlying the intellectuals' denunciation of injustice, in the end, is the passion of ambition, the desire to rule other men.[9] According to the classical political philosophers, this passion is very closely akin to the desire that leads to philosophy: the tyrant (in whom the desire to rule is most powerful) is a philosopher gone wrong.[10] Given the natural limitations of earthly existence, the life that combines perfect freedom and nobility can be attained only through contemplation rather than through praxis. The highest justification of the liberal regime is that it provides legal protection to those who would pursue such a life. But if philosophy is to be revived, her true character must once again be recognized.

APPENDIX
RAWLS'S "FAIRNESS TO GOODNESS"

In 1975 Rawls published an article entitled "Fairness to Goodness" which embodies the author's responses to some of the criticisms that had been made of his account of the original position in *A Theory of Justice.* Although Rawls makes no reference to my own articles criticizing his book (two of which had been published more than a year previously to Rawls's article), the two main criticisms he deals with are similar or identical to some arguments I made in those articles as well as in the present volume. Let us consider how far Rawls's article succeeds in answering these criticisms.

In "Fairness to Goodness" Rawls summarizes his endeavor as follows: "... I have tried to blunt the force of two objections to the idea of the original position: (a) that it incorrectly excludes morally relevant information [i.e., the parties' conceptions of the good]; and (b) that it is arbitrarily biased (given the motivation assumption and the nature of primary goods) in favor of individualistic conceptions of the good."[1]

I believe that Rawls fails in this endeavor, for the same reasons that he failed in his original attempt to deduce principles of justice from the original position. Some of Rawls's remarks in "Fairness to Goodness" are nonetheless of interest, for they make more explicit some of the problematic assumptions of the author's procedure which I have tried to point out in the preceding analysis.

One interesting point in "Fairness to Goodness" is the author's elaboration of the reasons underlying his inclusion of the veil of ignorance in constructing the original position, particularly his denial to the parties in the original position of knowledge of their conceptions of the good. As Rawls now explains,

There are . . . at least three different reasons for excluding information from the original position: it would permit self- and group-interest to distort the parties' deliberations; it refers to contingencies and accidents that should not influence the choice of moral principles; or it represents the very moral conceptions (or aspects thereof) that we seek to understand in the light of other and more basic notions.[2]

Of these three reasons, Rawls emphasizes the second as an explanation of why knowledge of the good must be excluded from the original position. According to Rawls, the fact "that we have one conception of the good rather than another is not relevant from a moral standpoint." The reason for this is that "our final ends . . . depend on our abilities and opportunities, on the numerous contingencies that have shaped our attachments and affections." In other words, men's opinions about what is good are inevitably determined by such arbitrary contingencies as "our social position and class, our sex and race, [which] should not influence deliberations made from a moral point of view. . . ."[3]

This explanation brings out as an aspect of the original position a feature of Rawls's thought that in *A Theory of Justice* itself (as I noted in chapter 4) did not emerge until part 3: his neo-Marxian notion of the social determination of all thought. The above argument is remarkable in that it denies the possibility that a person could *transcend* the biases produced by his social position, class, sex, or race and *objectively* determine what is good for himself, and for men generally, through the exercise of reason. Yet Rawls does not seem to recognize that this principle, if true, would apply equally against the supposed objectivity of his own account of justice.

Rawls tries to defend the objectivity of his procedure by observing "that people's conceptions of the right are also bracketed"—that is, concealed by the veil of ignorance—in the original position. But this defense is inadequate, for the following reason: the principles that emerge from the original position are to be *tested against* what Rawls calls "our considered judgments" of justice. In other words, Rawls's beliefs about justice are not, in the end, bracketed. But since Rawls has held that men's judgments about what is good are inevitably biased by the contingencies of their particular condition, the same would seem to be true of their beliefs about justice. Thus there is no reason to assume that the considered judgments that the principles of justice are supposed to explicate have any objective validity. Nor, consequently, has Rawls given an adequate justification of why men's conceptions of the good should be bracketed in determining the principles of justice.

This brings us to the second objection with which Rawls proposes to deal in "Fairness to Goodness:" the argument that the original position is arbitrarily biased in favor of a particular view of the good. Rawls's response to this charge contains the most interesting admission of the article. In *A Theory of Justice* itself Rawls claimed that the original position embodied "no restrictive assumptions about the parties' conceptions of the good except that they are rational long-term plans" (129). But, returning to this problem near the end of the book, he remarked: "I do not hold that the conception of the original position is itself without moral force, or that the family of concepts it draws upon is ethically neutral. This question I simply leave aside" (579).

In "Fairness to Goodness," discarding his former reticence, Rawls now admits openly: "The original position is certainly not neutral in the sense that its description uses no moral concepts. . . . And, of course, the original position as a whole is not neutral between conceptions of the good in the sense that the principles of justice adopted permit them all equally. Any definite agreement is bound to favor some conceptions over others."[4]

But if the original position is in fact structured so as to favor some conceptions of the good over others, what justification remains for denying to the parties in that position a knowledge of their own particular conceptions of the good, so that they could determine the meaning of justice in that light? Rawls's answer is that while the original position is not neutral among conceptions of the good, it is supposed to be fair to them. However, "Even this may be asking too much, since there may be no very clear notion of fairness for this case or, at any rate, no notion of perfect fairness." It is still possible to argue that "the original position is as fair as possible," however, by looking at it as an attempt "to work out principles of accommodation between different moralities much as a constitution insuring liberty of conscience and freedom of thought contains principles of accommodation between different religions."[5]

This analogy between Rawls's procedure and the means by which liberal constitutions have been established is not a satisfactory one, however, for reasons that have already been suggested in chapters 2 and 3. The establishment of such constitutions did not rest on an abstract principle of fairness to all religions and moralities, but rather on a particular and explicit view of the human good to which all parties agreed, according to which the claims of life, liberty, and the pursuit of happiness, to use the words of the Declaration of Independence, take precedence over any particular religious claims that contradict them. It was only as a result of the prior settlement of the religious question through the weakening of religious sentiment that the principle of toleration could be agreed on.[6]

What prevents Rawls from justifying his principles in the same way is, as we have seen, his insistence that the just cannot be derived from the good. In other words, even while admitting that his construction of the original position favors some conceptions of the good over others, he refuses to allow the parties in the original position to evaluate those conceptions against alternative ones as a basis for choosing principles of justice. But he thereby undermines any ground for demonstrating that men should come to agreement on such principles—except his unsupported claim that such agreement is required by men's sense of justice.

Rawls nonetheless undertakes to defend the "fairness," if not the neutrality, of the original position as regards conceptions of the good by refuting the charge that his "assumptions about primary goods . . . bias the choice of principles in an individualistic direction and against communitarian values."[7] His major arguments are as follows:

1. Since some amount of wealth is needed for the accomplishment of any plan of life, calling wealth a primary good is consistent with approving of various ways of life and modes of social organization. "The desire for income and wealth . . . understood as the (legal) command over exchangeable means for satisfying human needs and interests, is characteristic of societies generally. It is not peculiar to societies in which people have individualistic rather than communitarian values."[8]

2. Since "the motivation assumption" of mutual disinterest holds only for the original position, there is no reason to assume that a society based on the two principles will itself consist of "self-interested individuals with individualistic aims." Quite the contrary: a plausible psychological assumption suggests that people in such a society will be less materialistic and selfish than they are at present, since

a just distribution of primary goods so affects human motives that under a just distribution people are less concerned with acquiring a greater index of these goods and concentrate for the most part on pursuing other aims within the framework that just institutions establish. Here one is assuming, as a general psychological fact, that strong or inordinate desires for more primary goods, . . . particularly a desire for greater income and wealth and prerogatives of position, spring from insecurity and anxiety. . . . To the extent that just institutions alleviate these psychological conditions, they reduce the strength of the quest for wealth and position.

3. The only conceptions of the good that would be excluded in a just society are those which either are "in direct conflict with the principles of justice," such as goals which "require the repression of certain groups on, say, racial or ethnic perfectionist grounds," or else while admissible, nonetheless "fail to gain adherents under the social conditions of a well-ordered society": for example, a religion which "can survive only if it controls the machinery of state and practices effective intolerance." The

loss of such ways of life is of "no significance." But there is no reason that communitarian ways of life should suffer under such conditions, especially since "the basic liberties . . . secure the right of free movement between associations and smaller communities." "Communitarian aims may be pursued" within the framework of the "one collective aim supported by state power for the whole well-ordered society: namely, that it be a well-ordered society, a just society wherein the common conception of justice is publicly recognized. . . ."[9]

I believe that I have already refuted each of these arguments. Rawls's observation that some degree of wealth is necessary for the fulfillment of any plan of life (indeed, it is necessary for the bare preservation of life) completely passes over the fact that his principles of justice, and consequently his vision of the well-ordered society, embody no *limit* to the pursuit of wealth. Only some account of an objective human good transcending the primary ones could provide a ground for such limits.[10] The only such account Rawls attempts to provide—his discussion of self-respect and the ideal of social union in part 3—is much too vague and relativistic to supply such a ground. And, as I observed in chapter 3, Rawls's denial to the government of the authority to promote morality and religion through legislation makes it unlikely that such supra-material goods will be seriously pursued by the majority of a society.

Rawls's claim regarding the transformation that the institution of his principles of justice would work on human motivation is entirely speculative and wholly unsupported. As I have tried to show, the two principles in themselves are so vague that Rawls has no way of demonstrating that American society as it is presently constituted does not conform to them. A more serious argument could be made, I think, to show on non-Rawlsian grounds that the American regime is as just as any that has ever existed. Yet the justice, freedom, and prosperity that Americans enjoy are largely the product of the way that the American Constitution and the principles underlying it facilitate and encourage the widespread pursuit of material goods (rather than upholding a rigidly aristocratic class system, or encouraging the devotion to potentially less pacific goals such as religious salvation or national glory).[11] There is no evidence to suggest that policies—whatever they might be—designed to make this country conform better to Rawls's principles would reduce the degree of materialism and individualism in American life.

Rawls's explanation of the pursuit of superior wealth, power, and status as the product of insecurity and anxiety could have been taken straight from the mouth of Nietzsche's last man. It may be appealing to some men, but it is hardly persuasive, to explain the fact that they have achieved less renown than Caesar, or less wealth than J. Paul Getty, by reference to their superior psychic health. It would be more entertaining, and probably more enlightening, to speculate on how Caesar (to say nothing of Flaubert) might explain the psychic motives that underlie the popularity of *A Theory of Justice.*

It may well be—as so profound and balanced a thinker as Tocqueville appears to have concluded—that an egalitarian, commercial, individualistic regime like the American one is on the whole preferable to other sorts of society that tended to foster a greater degree of piety, civic virtue, and military and political greatness. But one cannot defend liberalism either by denying its essentially individualistic and materialistic tendencies, or by dismissing the lost greatness as having no significance.

NOTES

PREFACE

1. These studies include the four articles listed below. I am grateful to the publishers of each of the journals in which they appeared for allowing me to reprint considerable portions of these articles in the present volume:
"The 'Sense' and Non-Sense of Justice: An Examination of John Rawls's *A Theory of Justice,*" *Political Science Reviewer* 3 (1973): 1–41.
"A Critique of Rawls's Contract Doctrine," *Review of Metaphysics* 28, no. 1 (September, 1974): 89–115.
"Ideology in Philosophy's Clothing: John Rawls's *A Theory of Justice,*" *Georgia Political Science Association Journal* 4, no. 2 (fall, 1976): 35–57.
"'Moral Theory' versus Political Philosophy: Two Approaches to Justice," *Review of Politics* 39, no. 2 (April, 1977): 192–219.
2. For a lucid account of this transformation, cf. Hans Jonas, "The Practical Uses of Theory," *The Phenomenon of Life,* pp. 188–210.
3. In a recent popular article on the current state of philosophy, it is estimated that "there are more than 2,500 unemployed philosophers" in the United States alone. (One suggested remedy for this problem is that business corporations each be persuaded to hire a house philosopher.) According to this article, the philosophers themselves do not regard their state as a prosperous one—not only because of the specter of unemployment, but also because of the low esteem in which their discipline is held by non-philosophers. This lack of esteem is no doubt partly due to the isolation to which philosophical scholars are reported to believe their discipline commits them. (Taylor Branch, "New Frontiers in American Philosophy.")

INTRODUCTION

1. Alexis de Tocqueville, *Democracy in America,* 2.1.1.393. I have modified Lawrence's translation in this and other quotations from Tocqueville.
2. *The Liberal Tradition in America,* p. 10.
3. These essays appeared, respectively, in the April, 1972, issue of the *Yale Law Journal;* the November, 1974, issue of the *Quarterly Journal of Economics;* and the June, 1975, issue of the *American Political Science Review.*

4.   David K. Hart, "Social Equity, Justice, and the Equitable Administrator," p. 3.
5.   Norman Daniels (ed.), *Reading Rawls,* introduction, p. xi (emphasis in original).
6.   Review of *A Theory of Justice,* pp. 1, 18.
7.   "A New Philosophy of the Just Society," pp. 34–39.
8.   "Justice Deserted, or What Is Really Wrong with Rawls," p. 1.
9.   *The Liberal Theory of Justice,* p. ix.
10.   *Anarchy, State, and Utopia,* p. 183.
11.   "Social Evaluation through Notional Choice," p. 597.
12.   P. 37.
13.   P. 1. Daniels, p. xi, similarly observes that "many readers and editors found in Rawls's work a welcome return to an older tradition of substantive, rather than semantic moral and political philosophy."
14.   For evidence of the continuing scholarly interest in Rawls's work, see the chronological bibliography of studies on it compiled by Robert K. Fullinwider, *Political Theory,* vol. 5, no. 4 (November, 1977), pp. 561–570. See also the review by Garry Wills of some recent books on ethics, "Ethical Problems," which praises recent works by Charles Fried and Sissela Bok for "help[ing] us read our Rawls," and concludes that "reading Mr. Rawls helps us in the endless task of maintaining those taboos that guard both individual dignity and social solidarity." (*New York Times Book Review,* June 25, 1978, p. 13).

1. POLITICAL PHILOSOPHY AND THE SENSE OF JUSTICE

1.   Daniels, p. xi.
2.   Ibid., p. xii.
3.   "A New Philosophy of the Just Society," p. 34. A similar claim is made by Marshall Cohen, review of *A Theory of Justice,* p. 1. Sidney S. Alexander, "Social Evaluation through Notional Choice," p. 602, on the other hand, denies that Rawls is practicing "ordinary language philosophy." I discuss Rawls's relation to the ordinary-language movement in chapter 5.
4.   All page references in parentheses within the text are to *A Theory of Justice.*
5.   Hence Leon H. Craig, for instance, while critical of Rawls's position, appears in one of his articles on Rawls to accept (as Cohen does, from a more sympathetic point of view) Rawls's claim to represent the social contract tradition and the principles of liberalism. ("Contra Contract," pp. 63, 81.) Similarly, Robert Nisbet treats Rawls as "without question, a lineal descendant of Rousseau" ("The Pursuit of Equality," p. 108).
6.   According to Taylor Branch, "New Frontiers in American Philosophy," the prevailing view among analytic philosophers "is that . . . philosophy was always too difficult for anyone but the specialist." The unerotic character of the philosophical discipline understood in this manner is suggested by Branch's account of the views of a leading contemporary logician, Saul Kripke: "Kripke believes that philosophers do not escape their desires entirely; they only suppress them" (pp. 62–63). Compare Plato, *Republic* 581b–e, *Banquet* 210c–d; Nietzsche, *Beyond Good and Evil,* part 6 and sec. 295.
7.   Pp. xii–xiv.
8.   P. xiv.
9.   Aristotle, *Nicomachean Ethics* 1098b6–7.
10.   "On Classical Political Philosophy," *What Is Political Philosophy?* pp. 78, 80.
11.   Cf. Harry V. Jaffa, "Aristotle," p. 95: "What is most significant about Aristotle's method in Book III is . . . that it draws philosophic conclusions from the opinions of men who are neither philosophers nor legislators, but men who are contending for political advantages in political life."

12.   As noted by Brian Barry, *The Liberal Theory of Justice,* p. 1; and by Robert Paul Wolff, *Understanding Rawls,* pp. 1–3.

13.   In "The Independence of Moral Theory," his 1974 presidential address delivered to the annual meeting of the American Philosophical Association and published in that association's *Proceedings,* Rawls describes moral theory as a central part, rather than the whole, of moral philosophy (p. 5), and distinguishes this part as follows:

> Moral theory is the study of substantive moral conceptions, that is, the study of how the basic notions of the right, the good, and moral worth may be arranged to form different moral structures. Moral theory tries to identify the chief similarities and differences between these structures and to characterize the way in which they are related to our moral sensibilities and natural attitudes, and to determine the conditions they must satisfy if they are to play their expected role in human life.

According to the understanding that Rawls sets forth in this article, the scope of moral theory is smaller than that of moral philosophy, in that the moral theorist "put[s] aside the idea of constructing a correct theory of right and wrong, that is, a systematic account of what we regard as objective moral truths." It is desirable at least provisionally to "bracket the problem of moral truth," Rawls believes, because "the history of moral philosophy shows that the notion of moral truth is problematical." If progress is to be achieved in moral philosophy, analogous to that which has been accomplished in logic during the past century, it is necessary that the moral theorist separate his role "as an observer . . . of other people's moral conceptions and attitudes" from his "role as someone who has a particular conception" of morality (pp. 6–7). The problematical character of moral truth can be transcended by concentrating on "the comparative study of moral conceptions" held by men, without regard to the question of the truth of those conceptions (p. 21).

Although Rawls does not expressly acknowledge this fact, his definition of moral theory in "The Independence of Moral Theory" seems to be considerably narrower than, and even in contradiction with, the understanding of moral theory that is embodied in *A Theory of Justice.* As I have noted in the text, Rawls proposes in *A Theory of Justice* to set forth an account of justice that would reduce or even eliminate men's disagreements about justice; such an enterprise seems to involve considerably more than an exercise in "the comparative study of moral conceptions." Moreover, Rawls expressly proposes in the book to investigate the *soundness* of men's intuitive beliefs about justice: he is not therefore bracketing the issue of moral truth.

Rawls's redefinition of his enterprise in the later article seems to represent a retreat from the claims set forth in *A Theory of Justice,* perhaps out of a thus far unacknowledged recognition on his part of some of the epistemological difficulties that I raise in chapters 1 and 5, as well as difficulties in defending his substantive understanding of justice against the criticisms that have been levelled against it from both the left and the right. But to limit the claims of moral theory in this way is surely to reduce its interest: as I note in the introduction, much of the popularity of *A Theory of Justice* has stemmed from the belief that it represents a revival of substantive moral and political philosophy, rather than one more academic exercise in "the comparative study of moral conceptions." Nor is it at all evident that one can separate, as Rawls wants to, the role of moral observation from the substantive study of moral truth. Such a distinction embodies all the difficulties that have been encountered in positivistic social science, to which I allude in chapter 5.

14.   Plato, *Republic* 359b, 362a.

15.   Starting from premises seemingly akin to Rawls's, another contemporary exponent of moral theory, Richard W. Eggerman, suggests the likelihood that those premises point precisely to the truth of "ethical relativism." "Moral Theory and Practicality," pp. 175, 177n.

16.   "The Sense of Justice," p. 281.

17. In "The Independence of Moral Theory" Rawls so emphasizes the dependence of men's moral conceptions on their sentiments (p. 6) as to reject the very claim that those conceptions have any necessary objective validity: moral theory thus becomes "a kind of psychology and does not presuppose the existence of objective moral truths" (p. 9). As I have noted in footnote 13, supra, however, this more radical position seems to conflict with Rawls's claim in *A Theory of Justice* to provide an account of justice that *is* objective and hence can be agreed upon by men generally, regardless of the peculiarities of their individual sentiments or their upbringing.

18. "The Sense of Justice," p. 298.

19. *Émile,* 1.33–35.

2. THE ORIGINAL POSITION VERSUS THE STATE OF NATURE

1. Cf. R. M. Hare, "Rawls' Theory of Justice," p. 83.

2. Rawls, "Justice as Fairness."

3. In part 3 Rawls does assert that "dominant end" theories are "inhuman" (553). On his view, therefore, such men as Loyola (553), to say nothing of Plato and Aristotle, pursued inhuman ways of life, and the principles that guided them are less reflective of humanity than are the decisions of the artificial parties to Rawls's original position. Even if one could accept this unlikely consequence, Rawls's assertion would still not have proved anything regarding the relative rationality of the alternatives, particularly given the instrumental character of his understanding of rationality. In fact, Aristotle demonstrates in *Nicomachean Ethics* 1.1–2 that Rawls's view of life is the irrational one. Cf. also Plato, *Republic* 519b–c; Victor Gourevitch, "Rawls on Justice," pp. 499–501.

4. For a more thorough critique of the notion of instrumental rationality, cf. Herbert J. Storing, "The Science of Administration," in Storing (ed.), *Essays on the Scientific Study of Politics,* pp. 63–150.

5. The difficulties in Rawls's assumption are elaborated in Leon H. Craig, "Contra Contract," pp. 68–70.

6. I discuss this point further with reference to Aristotle's "natural right" teaching in chapter 5.

7. The formulation of the two principles cited here is Rawls's final and most specific one; there are several earlier versions.

8. Rawls is exceedingly vague throughout the book regarding the kind of social conditions that justify abrogating the priority of liberty. One might imagine him to be agreeing with John Stuart Mill's principle that liberty is actualizable only given a people's attainment of a certain level of civilization and education (John Stuart Mill, *On Liberty,* pp. 96–97). Rawls's remarks, however, that "the value of liberty depends upon circumstances" (247) and that "the fair value of political liberty" in particular is determined by "the distribution of property and wealth" (226) suggest something further: that men should not trouble themselves overly about liberty until more "basic" material needs are met. Perhaps this is intended as justification for the denial of liberty in such regimes as Maoist China. If so, it would help explain the absence of any criticism on Rawls's part of the Communist regimes for abridging liberty, even as he denounces "existing" (presumably Western) regimes for allowing excessive economic inequalities to persist (226, 279). Cf. Benjamin R. Barber, "Justifying Justice," p. 303n., which explicitly notes that Rawls's notion of a threshold for the priority of liberty is in principle compatible with Marxism. Cf. also the criticisms of the threshold argument made by Brian Barry, *The Liberal Theory of Justice,* pp. 74–77.

9. Rawls's reasoning on this point is so obscure, and the self-contradiction so manifest, that it seems appropriate to quote him at length here. Rawls represents the two principles as "the maximin solution to the problem of social justice" because

"the two principles are those which a person would choose for the design of a society in which *his enemy is to assign him his place*" (152; emphasis added). He then proceeds as follows:

The persons in the original position *do not, of course, assume that their initial place in society is decided by a malevolent opponent.* As I note below, they should not reason from false premises. The veil of ignorance does not violate this idea, since an absence of information is not misinformation. But that the two principles of justice would be chosen if the parties were forced to protect themselves against such a contingency explains the sense in which this conception is the maximin solution. And this analogy suggests that if the original position has been described so that it is rational for the parties to adopt the conservative attitude expressed by this rule, a conclusive argument can indeed be constructed for these principles. Clearly the maximin rule is not, in general, a suitable guide for choices under uncertainty. But it is attractive in situations marked by certain special features. My aim, then, is to show that a good case can be made for the two principles based on the fact that *the original position manifests these features to the fullest possible degree, carrying them to the limit,* so to speak. [153; emphasis added]

Of course, Rawls has not at all designed the original position so as to manifest the features that would make the maximin rule an appropriate guide: he has denied that the parties feel envy or hostile feelings towards one another, has assumed that their fundamental needs are complementary, and has attributed to them a sense of justice that effectively regulates their conduct towards one another. Rawls's contradiction on this point arises out of a conflict between his individualism and his communitarianism that I discuss further on in chapter 2 and also in chapter 4.

10. Moreover, as Barry points out (p. 97), the argument contradicts the assumption, implicit in the difference principle, that the prospect of achieving primary goods *above* the minimum acts as an effective incentive to men to exert themselves in ways that incidentally benefit the less advantaged.

11. The dubiousness of Rawls's purported demonstration that his two principles would be chosen over utilitarianism in the original position is demonstrated at length by David Lyons, "Nature and Soundness of the Contract and Coherence Arguments."

12. This fact has also been noted by Sidney S. Alexander, "Social Evolution through Notional Choice," p. 604; and Barry, p. 13.

13. On the secularist, materialistic bias of the original position, cf. Craig, pp. 73–74, 77; Robert Paul Wolff, *Understanding Rawls,* p. 75; Barber, pp. 313–14; Gourevitch, pp. 489–90, 497. Rawls attempts to refute the charge that his two principles embody a materialistic bias in a 1975 article entitled "Fairness to Goodness." I examine this article, and attempt to show that Rawls's defense against the charge fails, in the appendix.

14. With respect to Locke, consider especially chapter 9 of his *Second Treatise;* also, Leo Strauss, *Natural Right and History,* pp. 202–34; Robert Goldwin, "John Locke," pp. 452–60; Richard H. Cox, *Locke on War and Peace* chap. 2; C. B. Macpherson, *The Political Theory of Possessive Individualism,* pp. 240–41. For Rousseau, see *Discourse on the Origin and Foundations of Inequality,* in *First and Second Discourses,* p. 157, regarding the character of human relations immediately prior to the institution of government. Kant's Hobbism comes out clearly in his "Perpetual Peace," pp. 92, 99–100, 110–12.

15. I discuss this contradiction further in chapter 4.

16. On the differences between Rawls's primary goods and Hobbes's "power," however, cf. Allan Bloom, "Justice," p. 654; Leon H. Craig, "Traditional Political Philosophy and John Rawls' Theory of Justice," pp. 34–36.

17. Cf. Harvey C. Mansfield, Jr., "Hobbes and the Science of Indirect Government." Consider also Rousseau's analogy of the statue of Glaucus in the preface to the *Discourse on the Origin and Foundations of Inequality,* p. 91.

18.   Craig, "Traditional Political Philosophy," puts the point nicely: "Hobbes threatens you with death. Rawls threatens to call you unjust" (p. 39).

19.   For Hobbes's demonstration of this point, consider *Leviathan,* chap. 13, with the reasoning for the ninth law of nature in chap. 15; cf. also Joseph Cropsey, "Hobbes and the Transition to Modernity," *Political Philosophy and the Issues of Politics,* pp. 303-4.

20.   At p. 33 Rawls expressly exempts Locke and Hume from his criticism of the utilitarians. He does not explain why he nonetheless chooses to compare his theory with that of the utilitarians, rather than with the seemingly sounder views of Locke and Hume. Indeed, he does not explain why it is necessary to go beyond Locke and Hume at all. Compare Aristotle, *Politics* 1260b28-36, 1268a6-10.

3. JUST INSTITUTIONS

1.   It is highly significant that Rawls, in demanding that the principles of justice be determined prior to the institution of government, reverses Hobbes's order. This reversal, which severs justice from prudence, exemplifies the doctrinairism of Rawls's approach. As Irving Kristol has observed, Rawls obliterates the distinction between the best and the legitimate, effectively denying legitimacy to all regimes that may be prevented by circumstances (if not by good sense) from actualizing his principles. Hobbes would say that this amounts to an incitement to anarchy. See Irving Kristol, "About Equality," p. 42; Hobbes, *Leviathan,* chap. 15, p. 94; chap. 29, p. 211.

2.   Rawls's narrow conception of the political process as a machine wholly distinct from the judicial process strikingly resembles the discredited mechanical account of judicial review, according to which constitutional interpretations are entirely separable from judgments of policy. Contrast Hamilton, Madison, and Jay, *Federalist,* p. 528, regarding the exercise of judicial prudence; also Alexander M. Bickel, *The Least Dangerous Branch,* especially Bickel's remark on p. 70 regarding the need for the Supreme Court to test "basic principles . . . in the concrete circumstances of a case." This need is reflected in the Court's "case and controversy" rule, which leads it to avoid considering sham cases that do not involve an actual, particular controversy between opposed parties.

3.   Cf. *A Theory of Justice,* pp. 270-74; "Fairness to Goodness," p. 546; Allan Bloom, "Justice," p. 649; Benjamin R. Barber, "Justifying Justice," pp. 312-13; Brian Barry, *The Liberal Theory of Justice,* p. 166.

4.   Cf. *Federalist,* no. 10; Martin Diamond, Winston M. Fisk, and Herbert Garfinkel, *The Democratic Republic,* pp. 75-80; Thomas S. Schrock, "The Liberal Court, the Conservative Court, and Constitutional Jurisprudence"; Milton Friedman, *Capitalism and Freedom,* chap. 1; Joseph Cropsey, *Polity and Economy* pp. x, 71-72, 79, 94-98.

5.   Cf. the criticism of Rawls's argument on this ground in C. B. Macpherson, *Democratic Theory,* pp. 89-94; also Barber, pp. 312-13.

6.   Cf. Leon H. Craig, "Contra Contract," pp. 73-74.

7.   Cf. George Washington, "Farewell Address," *The Writings of George Washington,* 35. 229; David Lowenthal, "Connecting Church and State Constitutionally"; Harvey C. Mansfield, Jr., "Thomas Jefferson," pp. 37-38; Harry M. Clor, *Obscenity and Public Morality,* pp. 186-209; Jean-Jacques Rousseau, *Politics and the Arts;* Victor Gourevitch, "Rawls on Justice," pp. 494-95; Glen E. Thurow, *Abraham Lincoln and American Political Religion.*

8.   On Adam Smith's use of the principle of religious liberty as a means of weakening the power of religion, cf. Cropsey, pp. 79-86. Cf. also Montaigne, *Essays* 2.19.509.

9.   Consider Thomas More's approach to the church-state problem as described in Richard G. Stevens, "The New Republic in More's *Utopia*"; and the opinion of the King of Brobdingnag in Swift's *Gulliver's Travels*, 2.6.106.

10.   Cf. Bloom, "Justice," pp. 653-54; Gourevitch, p. 498.

11.   *Social Contract*, book 2, chaps. 7, 9-11; book 3, chaps. 4, 14-15; book 4, chaps. 7-8; and the dedication to the *Discourse on the Origin and Foundations of Inequality;* also, Walter F. Berns, "The New Left and Liberal Democracy," pp. 26-28.

12.   Cf. especially the *Federalist,* no. 9, first paragraph.

13.   For a consideration of the kind of issues with which Rawls fails to consider in endorsing the doctrinaire principle of one man, one vote, cf. Robert Horwitz, "Reapportionment in Hawaii"; Harvey C. Mansfield, Jr., "Impartial Representation." With respect to the issue of how far political parties can or should be principled, or represent distinctive conceptions of the public good, cf. Harry V. Jaffa, "The Nature and Origin of the American Party System"; Edward C. Banfield, "In Defense of the American Party System"; and Joseph Cropsey, "Conservatism and Liberalism," in *Political Philosophy and the Issues of Politics,* pp. 116-30.

14.   The core of Kant's moral teaching as I have tried to summarize it here is contained in his *Foundations of the Metaphysic of Morals;* for his account of the just constitution, see the essay "Theory and Practice." A lucid exposition of Kant's political and moral teaching is set forth by Pierre Hassner, "Immanuel Kant."

15.   Cf. Bloom's discussion of Rawls's "denigration of the primary importance of generality or universality in Kant's thought" ("Justice," p. 656). Kant specifically infers from the principle of men's moral and legal equality that each man has a right to attain a position of honor that accords with his merit; to acquire an unlimited amount of wealth by legal means; and to bequeath his wealth to his heirs. See Kant, "Theory and Practice," pp. 417-19.

16.   Cf. Kant, "Theory and Practice," p. 419: one may bequeath material things as one wishes because these do not concern man's character. Cf. also Susan Meld Shell, "Kant's Theory of Property."

17.   Leon H. Craig, "Traditional Political Philosophy . . ." p. 41, rightly observes that "denying ethical significance to our natural differences does not establish the egalitarian premise, as Rawls seems to think. If these natural differences are morally neutral, as he claims, then they support *no* distributive principle, egalitarian or inegalitarian" (emphasis in original).

Michael P. Zuckert, "Justice Deserted: A Critique of John Rawls's *A Theory of Justice,*" brilliantly demonstrates that the understanding of justice embodied in Rawls's difference principle actually contradicts its alleged premise, the undeservedness of men's natural assets. Precisely because that premise undermines *any* criterion of desert and hence of justice, Zuckert points out, Rawls is compelled to shift from a desert model to an exchange model of justice in order to specify the criteria of just institutions. But Rawls's treatment of justice as an exchange, in which men's "different abilities are to be considered part of a common pool," and the possession of superior abilities and rewards by some is to be earned by their service to the less advantaged, is in turn undermined, Zuckert observes, by the defectiveness of the premise:

> . . . if possession by particular individuals does not prevent natural endowments and efforts from being part of a common pool, then there is no reason why possession by particular persons should prevent the goods from nonetheless belonging to the common pool as well. No matter what distribution of goods to individuals prevailed, "justice" would always be fulfilled, for the whole produces, and the whole possesses all. [p. 16]

(The paper by Zuckert that I have quoted here is a revised version of the paper that was cited in chapter 1.)

18.   At p. 512 Rawls explains that his theory of justice does not include an "account of . . . right conduct in regard to animals and the rest of nature," since "it does seem that we are not required to give strict justice anyway to creatures" lacking a sense of justice. An account "of our relations to animals and to nature would seem to depend upon a theory of the natural order and our place in it," and upon metaphysics. Rawls thus indicates his presupposition that man himself stands *outside* the natural order, and that an adequate account of human justice does not therefore depend upon an understanding of nature. The question I have posed in the text, however, remains unanswered: If the task of justice is to correct the arbitrariness of nature, why should we stop at redressing the inequality of human beings? Indeed, if nature has deprived the animals of a sense of justice, are men not then—on Rawls's assumption—obliged all the more to make them the greatest objects of their solicitude?

Obviously, once one begins to construct a moral theory founded solely in one's intuitions, and without regard to the character of nature, the possible consequences are limited only by a thinker's imagination—or by current intellectual fashions in the circles in which he travels. The step that Rawls stopped short of taking was taken, at least in part, by another philosophical scholar, Peter Singer (who has elsewhere criticized Rawls's reliance on intuition), in a book the thesis of which is aptly summarized by its title: *Animal Liberation.* In addition to setting forth a burning attack on "speciesism," Singer bridges the gap between theory and practice by appending a vegetarian cookbook designed to overcome "the tyranny of human over nonhuman animals" (p. vii).

For a critique of Singer's argument that stresses its deleterious consequences for the way that human beings treat one another, see the review by Marc F. Plattner in *Commentary.*

19.   Cf. Aristotle, *Nicomachean Ethics* 1131a15-29, *Politics* 3.12; Zuckert.

20.   Rawls uses this term at pp. 260 and 584 to signify his desire for a standard of justice independent of "the aims of existing individuals" (260); but since his fundamental objection is to the arbitrariness of nature as such, his real aspiration is to escape the natural order as a whole.

21.   Cf. the review of *A Theory of Justice* by Marshall Cohen in the *New York Times Book Review,* which surpasses Rawls himself in this regard while maintaining his dogmatic and self-righteous tone; Cohen denounces as unacceptable "the inequalities we now accept [and] the impairment of our liberties that we now endure," the "inglorious" character of our politics and the lack of "extravagant support" for our "high culture." It is not clear how Cohen would reconcile his desire to give "extravagant support" to high culture with his wish to eliminate "many economic and social inequalities, even if their elimination inhibits a further raising" of the general standard of living, for the sake of "a fuller participation in the common life" (p. 18).

22.   Cf. Christopher Jencks et al., *Inequality;* Daniel Bell, "On Meritocracy and Equality"; Seymour Martin Lipset, "Social Mobility and Equal Opportunity"; Rousseau, *Discourse on the Sciences and Arts,* in *First and Second Discourses,* p. 58; the *Federalist,* no. 10, sixth paragraph.

23.   *Democracy in America* 1.2.5.183 (emphasis added).

24.   Ibid., 2.2.13.510 (emphasis added).

25.   Cf. Berns, "The New Left . . . ," pp. 22–28; also Bertrand de Jouvenel's dissection of what he calls the "inner contradiction" of contemporary socialism, *The Ethics of Redistribution* pp. 11–14, 47–48.

26.   Cf. Aristotle, *Politics* 2.7, 3.9; Hobbes, *Leviathan,* chap. 14.

27.   Cf. Aristotle, *Politics* 2.1; the *Federalist,* no. 49; Abraham Lincoln, "On the Perpetuation of Our Political Institutions" (address to the Young Men's Lyceum of Springfield, Illinois, January 27, 1838), *Collected Works,* 1.108–15.

28. Cf. Herbert J. Storing, "The Case Against Civil Disobedience"; Harry V. Jaffa, "Reflections on Thoreau and Lincoln"; Steven R. Schlesinger, "Civil Disobedience"; Kant, "Theory and Practice," pp. 423–28.

4. THE MORALITY OF THE LAST MAN

1. Cf. also Rawls's review of Stephen Toulmin's *An Examination of the Place of Reason in Ethics,* in *Philosophical Review* 60 (1951), where Rawls seems (pp. 575–76) to endorse the distinction between ethical reasoning and "reasoning about the comparative worth of different ways of life as a whole," on the ground that the latter "are matters for personal, rather than ethical, decision."

2. "Justice," pp. 559–60.

3. Cf. also *A Theory of Justice,* p. 178: "Now our self-respect normally depends upon the respect of others. Unless we feel that our endeavors are honored by them, it is difficult if not impossible for us to maintain the conviction that our ends are worth pursuing."

4. Of course, Rawls unavoidably contradicts his own principle by calling some abilities "higher." At least so long as men persist in such usage, an inequality in the social esteem awarded to different kinds of abilities is inevitable.

5. Cf. Rawls's criticism of the democratic political process at p. 226 as "at best regulated rivalry." The degree of such rivalry will presumably be considerably reduced in Rawls's well-ordered society, thanks to its universal consensus about justice.

6. Plato, *Republic* 540e–541a. Cf. also Rawls's remark in his article "Fairness to Goodness," p. 543, regarding the need "to work out what conceptions of the good and what moral interests people would acquire" from living in "a well-ordered society," as distinguished from the beliefs and desires that presently characterize them.

Let me emphasize that I do not for a moment believe Rawls to be a conscious advocate of tyranny in any form. The actual political beliefs Rawls holds, as these are stated in part 2, are those of a loyal and decent (albeit rather simpleminded) liberal democrat. The problem is that the abstract egalitarianism to which Rawls also adheres conflicts with, and in part 3 ultimately predominates over, his liberalism. It is precisely the abstractness of Rawls's mode of argument that seems to prevent him from recognizing the implications of what he is saying; it is hard to believe, for instance, that Rawls really means what he says when he proposes the reconstitution of society in utter disregard of its present members' desires and beliefs; and his claim that all activities are equally deserving of esteem is contradicted, as I noted earlier, by his own reference to higher faculties.

Unfortunately, the innocence of an author's private intentions may not suffice to prevent his public teaching from having consequences that the author himself would later have cause to regret. As I have pointed out in the text, Rawls's doctrinaire egalitarianism, combined with his intemperate denunciations of the unjustness of existing liberal societies (to say nothing of his speculation about adopting "eugenic policies, more or less explicit" [107]), serves to encourage and justify dangerous and anti-liberal political prejudices. Even short of encouraging anti-liberal movements, Rawls's rhetoric, by challenging the fundamental legitimacy of liberal regimes as presently constituted, and encouraging disobedience to the laws of such regimes, tends to weaken his readers' support for those regimes. Rawls would have done better to consider, before propounding his theory, the advice of Montaigne to would-be political reformers: before acting, they should make very sure of the badness of what they are throwing out, and the goodness of what they are bringing in (*Essays* 1.23.88).

7. *Nicomachean Ethics* 1099a1–4, 1154b20–31, 1170a1–1170b14; also, Joseph Cropsey, "What Is Welfare Economics?" *Political Philosophy and the Issues of Politics,* pp. 22–25.

8. *Discourse on the Origin and Foundations of Inequality,* in *First and Second Discourses,* pp. 148–49, 155–56, 179, 221–22.

9. Cf. Allan Bloom, "Jean-Jacques Rousseau," pp. 550–52.

10. On Rawls's misinterpretation of Kant, cf. Bloom, "Justice," pp. 656–57; Oliver A. Johnson, "The Kantian Interpretation."

11. As Allan Bloom notes, although part of Kant's political teaching is contractuarian, his teaching about morality is not derived from a contract, as Rawls's principles of justice are (Bloom, "Justice," p. 656). Cf. also Leonard Choptiany, "A Critique of John Rawls's Principles of Justice"; Benjamin R. Barber, "Justifying Justice," pp. 315–18; Victor Gourevitch, "Rawls on Justice," p. 491n.

12. *Thus Spoke Zarathustra,* pp. 129–30.

13. Nowhere is the lack of seriousness in Rawls's conception of life more evident than in his example of a choice of plans of life: "planning a holiday" (551). Apparently unable to conceive of a dilemma more pressing than having to choose between seeing "the most famous church in Christendom and the most famous museum" (551), Rawls thereby avoids facing the serious issues that justice entails. Cf. Bloom, "Justice," p. 659; Barber, p. 310.

14. Marx's project for obliterating man's distinctively human capacities is stated most explicitly in the introduction to his "Contribution to the Critique of Hegel's *Philosophy of Right,*" which calls for the "total loss" of humanity for the sake of its alleged total redemption (p. 22). This project is said to entail the abolition of religion (12), the negation of philosophy (16), and the "struggle against [man's] own internal priest"–i.e., his conscience (18), as well as the obliteration of politics. (Page references are to *The Marx-Engels Reader,* ed. Robert C. Tucker). Marx's claim that communist society would, in compensation for these losses, liberate every man's potentiality to be creative is refuted by Nietzsche's infinitely profounder reflections on the subject of human excellence and creativity. See, especially, Nietzsche's *The Use and Abuse of History,* the second of the *Thoughts Out of Season;* and *Beyond Good and Evil,* part 9.

15. Cf. Locke, *Second Treatise,* chap. 5 (the relation between the invention of money and the productivity of agriculture); Harvey C. Mansfield, Jr., "Liberal Democracy As a Mixed Regime."

16. "Justice," p. 659.

17. Booker T. Washington, *Up from Slavery,* p. 16. See also Herbert J. Storing, "The School of Slavery," p. 68, where Storing contrasts Douglass's response to segregation with that of Martin Luther King, Jr., as expressed in the latter's *Stride toward Freedom.* King's conception of selfhood as entirely dependent on the regard of others, unlike the views not only of Douglass but of such more recent Black Power theorists as Malcolm X, strikingly resembles Rawls's.

18. Rawls's baldest statement of sociological determinism occurs in the article "Fairness to Goodness," where he contrasts his doctrine with that of "abstract individualism." Whereas the former holds "that the fundamental aims and interests of individuals are determined independently from particular social forms," with society and the state regarded as instrumental to "these antecedent individual ends and purposes," Rawls's "theory of a well-ordered society stresses," by contrast, "that the interests and ends of individuals depend upon existing institutions and the principles of justice they satisfy" (pp. 546–47). Cf. also Bloom, "Justice," pp. 659–60.

19. Cf. Aristotle, *Politics* 1267a2–16, *Nicomachean Ethics* 1155a22–28; Delba Winthrop, "Aristotle and Theories of Justice," p. 10, second paragraph.

20. *Nicomachean Ethics* 9.8. Cf. Joseph Cropsey, "'Alienation' or Justice?" *Political Philosophy and the Issues of Politics* p. 48.

21.   Further evidence of the anti-liberal tendency that Rawls's thought exemplifies and encourages is to be found in his exchange with R. A. Musgrave concerning the latter's proposal for "a lump sum tax on natural assets." Musgrave proposed such a tax in order to compel "recluses, saints, and (nonconsulting) scholars who earn but little . . . to allocate more of their time to income earning activities in order to contribute more to redistribution" ("Maximin, Uncertainty, and the Leisure Trade-Off," p. 632; Rawls, "Reply to Alexander and Musgrave," ibid., p. 654). Interestingly, Rawls raises no *moral* objection to this proposal. Rawls reassures those who might fear or detest its anti-liberal character that it "is not an interference with liberty until it infringes upon the basic liberties, although a fuller account of these is necessary in order to decide when this happens." Without providing such an account, Rawls is still confident that the proposal does not violate basic liberties; hence he has "no initial objection to Musgrave's scheme viewed from a theoretical standpoint," but merely mentions certain practical difficulties involved in attempting to establish it (Rawls, "Reply," pp. 654–55).

22.   "About Equality," p. 44.

23.   Cf. Daniel Bell, "On Meritocracy and Equality," pp. 40–42, 56–57.

24.   Tocqueville, *Democracy* 1.1.3.49–50; also John C. Koritansky, "Two Forms of the Love of Equality. . . ."

25.   Plato, *Republic* 343c–e.

5. MORAL THEORY VERSUS POLITICAL PHILOSOPHY

1.   Two leading critiques of behavioral political science on such grounds (among others) are Herbert J. Storing (ed.), *Essays on the Scientific Study of Politics,* and Charles A. McCoy and John Playford (eds.), *Apolitical Politics.*

2.   Cf. Leo Strauss, *Natural Right and History,* chap. 2; Martin Diamond, "The Dependence of Fact upon 'Value'"; Storing (ed.), passim.

3.   Leo Strauss, "An Epilogue," p. 327.

4.   For discussion of a related example of the way that an abstract, game theory approach leads to a misunderstanding of the political problem, cf. John Plamenatz's sensible criticism of Kenneth Arrow's treatment of democracy, in *Democracy and Illusion,* pp. 183–84.

5.   Such social contract theorists as Hobbes do, indeed, determine the purpose of government by starting from an account of the needs of men in a pre-political condition. But the outcome of their analyses is an assertion of the primary necessity that a sovereign authority be instituted, having the power to regulate the distribution of goods as the *common* peace and prosperity may require.

6.   Cf. Robert Paul Wolff, *Understanding Rawls,* p. 208; Benjamin R. Barber, "Justifying Justice," p. 673; Sidney S. Alexander, "Social Evaluation through Notional Choice," p. 607; Leon H. Craig, "Contra Contract," p. 77.

7.   Cf. Victor Gourevitch, "Rawls on Justice," pp. 493–94; Charles Frankel, "The New Egalitarianism and the Old," pp. 56–57. Consider also Aristotle, *Politics* 1281a29–34 and 1283b40ff., where it is argued that even the claims of virtue must be moderated in the light of the common good. As for the more radical Nietzschean view that Rawls considers as another statement of the principle of perfection (325), it raises a question about the *possibility* of a true common good, and hence of justice, that cannot adequately be answered by an appeal to Rawls's sense of justice. Cf. Nietzsche, *Beyond Good and Evil,* sec. 43; *Thus Spoke Zarathustra,* 1.5.

8.   William L. McBride, "Social Theory *Sub Specie Aeternitatis,*" p. 987 (summarizing the view expressed by Stuart Hampshire in his previously cited review).

9.   The disagreement among Rawls's critics regarding the extent of Rawls's egalitarianism—some, like Nisbet, viewing him as a radical egalitarian, others, like Barber and Macpherson, charging that he tends to be a conservative defender of the status quo—is largely the result, I believe, of their concentrating on various parts of

A Theory of Justice. The grounds on which Rawls argues for the difference principle, combined with his occasional denunciations of existing injustices, encourage the belief that he is indeed some sort of radical; but the actual content of the two principles, as I have tried to show, points to no particular political consequences, while Rawls's specific prescriptions for political and economic institutions are roughly in accordance with the current editorial position of the *New York Times.*

10.   "Rawls' Theory of Justice," p. 83. Cf. also Leon H. Craig, "Traditional Political Philosophy," pp. 13–15; Peter Singer, "Philosophers Are Back on the Job," p. 19.

11.   According to Hare's count, there are "thirty expressions implying a reliance on intuitions" within a mere two pages of *A Theory of Justice* (Hare, p. 84).

12.   Cf. Craig, "Traditional Political Philosophy," pp. 12–17.

13.   Cf. Plato, *Phaedo* 99d–e; Walter F. Berns, "The Behavioral Sciences and the Study of Political Things," p. 557; Stanley Rosen, *Nihilism* pp. 149–56; Strauss, *Natural Right and History,* pp. 124–25.

14.   *Republic* 514a–518b.

15.   P. 83.

16.   Cf., in addition to the references in note 13 above, Plato, *Statesman* 285d–286a.

17.   *Nicomachean Ethics* 1098b9–12.

18.   Ibid. 1179a3–30.

19.   Cf. Strauss, *Natural Right and History,* pp. 124–25.

20.   For Aristotle's account of the supremacy of the philosophical life, cf. *Nicomachean Ethics* 10.7–8. On the gap between the views of most men and those of wise men: ibid. 1179a12–16.

21.   Cf. Aristotle, *Politics* 1280a9–22.

22.   *Posterior Analytics,* transl. G. R. G. Mure, in McKeon (ed.), *The Basic Works of Aristotle,* 71b20–21, 100b10–15.

23.   *Nicomachean Ethics* 1143b2–4.

24.   Cf. Harry V. Jaffa, *Thomism and Aristotelianism,* pp. 185–86.

25.   *Nicomachean Ethics,* transl. Ross, in *The Basic Works of Aristotle,* 1134b28–29, 1140a3–35; Jaffa, *Thomism,* pp. 179–83; Strauss, *Natural Right and History,* pp. 157–63.

26.   Cf. Jaffa, *Thomism,* pp. 171–87.

27.   Rawls, "Outline," p. 196; cf. Oliver A. Johnson, "The Kantian Interpretation."

28.   Cf. Plato, *Republic* 429b–c; Aristotle, *Nicomachean Ethics* 2.1, *Politics* 1269a20–22, *Metaphysics* 995a2–5; Montaigne, *Essays* 1.23.

29.   On the particular character of the American regime as it is presently constituted, cf. Joseph Cropsey, "The United States as Regime and the Sources of the American Way of Life," *Political Philosophy and the Issues of Politics,* pp. 1–15.

30.   *Nicomachean Ethics* 1.4, 1095b4–13; 2.1, 1103a14–20; 2.4, 1105b1–4; 5.9, 1137a9–12; 6.13, 1144b1–32; 10.7–8.

31.   *Republic* 514a–515c. The *Euthyphro* and the *Hipparchus,* along with Socrates' examination of Cephalus and Polemarchus in book 1 of the *Republic,* may be cited as instances of Plato's demonstration of the inadequacy, from the highest point of view, of the merely conventional morality. What Socrates' interlocutors in these cases lack is not merely an adequate theory of morality; their "intuitive" beliefs, derived from convention, but also biased (as almost all men's are) by their particular self-interests, are shown to lead, potentially or actually, to a substantively deficient manner of conduct.

32.   *The Prince,* chap. 11, first two sentences, and chap. 15. Cf. also Aristotle, *Politics* 2.8; Montaigne, *Essays* 3.1.

33.   The broader claim of utilitarianism that the good is equivalent to the useful does indeed raise substantive issues. But Rawls never considers these issues, because (as his account of the primary goods indicates) he agrees with the original utilitarians

regarding the content of goodness and differs only about the criteria according to which good things should be allocated among men. Cf. also the quotation from Warnock in the following footnote.

34. *Beyond Good and Evil,* sec. 228, p. 157. Consider also in this regard Mary Warnock's observation of the "surprising" character of the hostility expressed towards utilitarianism by "English empirical philosophers, many of whom would in their nonphilosophical moments turn out to be utilitarians of an enlightened liberal kind" (Warnock, *Ethics since 1900,* p. 140). The explanation of this paradox lies, one suspects, in the desire of such scholars to make the rather prosaic morality of bourgeois society appear noble because "altruistic."

35. "Justice as Fairness," p. 164; cf. also "Constitutional Liberty and the Concept of Justice."

36. Rawls rather unhelpfully suggests that his shift is due to the influence of "Burton Dreben, who made W. V. Quine's view clear to me and persuaded me that the notions of meaning and analyticity play no essential role in moral theory as I conceive of it" (*A Theory of Justice,* p. xi). One wishes that Rawls had been more explicit about the way in which he thinks Quine's writings serve to justify his procedure. Hare, for one ("Rawls' Theory of Justice," p. 83) denies that Quine's thought provides such a justification.

37. Cf. Ludwig Wittgenstein, *Philosophical Investigations,* secs. 90, 124, 126, 371; and Rosen, chap. 1. Allan Janik and Stephen Toulmin's study *Wittgenstein's Vienna* is of interest because of the light it sheds on the intentions and the self-understanding of the thinker who laid down the fundamental presuppositions of the contemporary ordinary-language school. The authors stress the way in which Wittgenstein's empiricist and largely apolitical English disciples failed to recognize the particular ethical intention underlying his doctrine (21–22). They also emphasize how Wittgenstein endeavored to *close off* certain lines of questioning by philosophers (pp. 221, 226, 261); the contrast with Socrates in this regard is striking. Compare Rawls: "Once the whole arrangement [of just institutions] is set up and going, *no questions are asked* about the totals of satisfaction or perfection" (*A Theory of Justice,* p. 161 [emphasis added]). Given Wittgenstein's restricted conception of the philosophic enterprise, one should not be surprised to learn of the limited, perhaps subordinate, importance he attached to it (Janik and Toulmin, pp. 207, 215, 219–20). Cf. Nietzsche, *Beyond Good and Evil,* sec. 204; and note 6 to chapter 1, supra.

These criticisms of the ordinary-language approach are not meant to deny that its abler practitioners sometimes produce sound and useful work. But such analysis can furnish only a beginning point for philosophy (as it does for instance, in Aristotle's writings), not its completion. The presupposition of Wittgenstein and his followers that it is impossible to transcend the grammar or the "form of life" of a particular people constitutes, as Rosen demonstrates, a form of historicism—a denial that an objective, transhistorical, transcultural account of the whole, or therefore of the human good, can be attained through reason. On Wittgenstein's historicism, cf. also Janik and Toulmin, pp. 231–32, 245. On the nature of historicism, cf. Strauss, *What Is Political Philosophy?* pp. 26–27, 56–77; Eugene Miller, "Positivism, Historicism, and Political Inquiry." For an analysis of the historicist presuppositions and implications of the thought of Rawls's acknowledged mentor, Quine, cf. Raymond L. Weiss, "Historicism and Science."

38. Thus G. E. Moore, after arguing that the nature of the good cannot be subjected to rational analysis, neatly solves the fundamental problem of ethics by pointing to the "obvious" truth that "the most valuable things . . . [are] the pleasures of human intercourse and the enjoyment of beautiful objects" (*Principia Ethic,* p. 188). Similarly, a more recent writer, T. D. Weldon, having dismissed the theoretical foundations of liberal democracy, such as the notion of natural rights, as "worthless," proceeds to suggest the substitution of an "empirical" test of

government that only a liberal democracy could pass. He admits, however, that this is merely a "personal view, or prejudice if that word is preferred"; unlike Rawls, he acknowledges that such a preference "has nothing philosophical about it" (*The Vocabulary of Politics* pp. 14, 87–101, 176).

39.   Cf. Warnock's criticism of the failure of previous generations of "moral philosophers in England to commit themselves to any moral opinions," and what turned out to be her well-founded optimism that this would soon change (*Ethics since 1900*, pp. 144–45). Responding to such exhortations, Janik and Toulmin, for instance, conclude their study of Wittgenstein by mocking "attempts to impose conventional standards of sexual morality by legal or political means" and suggesting the need for revision in the outdated "constitutional arrangements of 1776" (pp. 264, 270).

40.   Cf. Montaigne, *Essays* 3.4.

41.   Cf. Miller.

42.   "Justice," p. 659.

43.   See note 37, supra.

44.   "Fairness to Goodness," p. 546, as well as Rawls's notion of a threshold for the value of political liberty, discussed in chapter 2.

EPILOGUE

1.   "The New Egalitarianism and the Old," p. 55.

2.   Cf. Kristol's observation regarding the unawareness by academics and professionals of their own upper class status, "About Equality," p. 43.

3.   This is reflected in the fact, as noted by Victor Gourevitch ("Rawls on Justice," p. 489), that "Rawls concentrates on justice as a virtue of rules and institutions to the almost total exclusion of justice as a virtue of individuals." It is much more appealing to contemporary readers to attack the injustice of institutions, or of the distribution of wealth, than to remind them of the importance of individual morality. Cf. also George Benson and Thomas Engeman, *Amoral America*, p. 12; Irving Kristol, "Republican Virtue vs. Servile Institutions"; David L. Schaefer, "Democratic Statesmanship and Morality."

4.   For two recent illustrations, cf. Midge Decter, "Looting and Liberal Racism"; P. T. Bauer, "Western Guilt and Third World Poverty." The classic treatment of the subject, of course, is Tom Wolfe, *Radical Chic & Mau-Mauing the Flak Catchers.* On the related deficiencies of compassion as a political principle, cf. Clifford Orwin (University of Toronto), "Compassion as a Source of Democratic Morals."

5.   For a series of critiques of these policies, see my anthology *The New Egalitarianism.*

6.   "Capitalism, Socialism, and Nihilism," pp. 11–12; "About Equality," p. 45.

7.   Cf. Locke, *Second Treatise,* chap. 5.

8.   Kristol, "About Equality," p. 44.

9.   Cf. Kristol, "About Equality," pp. 43, 45; Harvey C. Mansfield, Jr., "Liberal Democracy as a Mixed Regime," pp. 10–12.

10.   Plato, *Republic* 491e–493a; Aristotle, *Politics* 1267a 10–14. Cf. also Leo Strauss, *On Tyranny,* especially chap. 5.

APPENDIX: Rawls's "Fairness to Goodness"

1.   P. 547.

2.   Ibid., p. 538.

3.   Ibid., p. 537.

4.   Ibid., p. 539.

5.   Ibid.

6.   Cf. Harvey C. Mansfield, Jr., "Party Government and the Settlement of 1688"; also "Thomas Jefferson," p. 37 (Jefferson's distinction regarding the relative desirability of differences of opinion over religious and political principles).

7.   "Fairness to Goodness," p. 540.

8.   Ibid., p. 541.

9.   Ibid., p. 550.

10.   Recall that Rawls raises no objection of principle to Musgrave's proposal to tax "recluses, saints, and (nonconsulting) scholars" so as to compel them to "allocate more of their time to income-earning activities in order to contribute more to redistribution" (see note 21 to chapter 4, supra). While conforming to the general spirit of Rawls's egalitarianism, such a proposal hardly promises to make society less materialistic.

11.   Cf. Martin Diamond, "Democracy and *The Federalist*," pp. 62–67.

BIBLIOGRAPHY

Note: In the case of classic philosophic works originally published prior to the twentieth century, I have provided a bibliographic reference only where a particular edition or translation was cited in the text.

Alexander, Sidney S. "Social Evaluation through Notional Choice." *Quarterly Journal of Economics* 88, no. 4 (November, 1974): 597–624.
Banfield, Edward C. "In Defense of the American Party System." Goldwin (ed.), *Political Parties, U. S. A.,* pp. 21–40.
Barber, Benjamin R. "Justifying Justice: Problems of Psychology, Politics, and Measurement in Rawls." Daniels (ed.), *Reading Rawls,* pp. 292–318.
Barry, Brian. *The Liberal Theory of Justice.* London: Oxford University Press, 1973.
Bauer, P. T. "Western Guilt and Third World Poverty." *Commentary* 61, no. 1 (January, 1976): 31–38.
Bell, Daniel. "On Meritocracy and Equality." *The Public Interest* 29 (fall, 1972): 29–68.
Benson, George C. S., and Thomas S. Engeman. *Amoral America.* Stanford, Calif.: Hoover Institution Press, 1975.
Berns, Walter F. "The Behavioral Sciences and the Study of Political Things." *American Political Science Review* 55, no. 3 (September, 1961): 550–59.
–––. "The New Left and Liberal Democracy." Goldwin (ed.), *How Democratic Is America?* pp. 17–38.
Bickel, Alexander, M. *The Least Dangerous Branch.* Indianapolis and New York: Bobbs-Merrill, 1962.
Bloom, Allan. "Justice: John Rawls vs. the Tradition of Political Philosophy." *American Political Science Review* 69, no. 2 (June, 1975): 648–62.
–––. "Jean-Jacques Rousseau." Strauss and Cropsey (eds.), *History of Political Philosophy,* pp. 532–53.
Branch, Taylor. "New Frontiers in American Philosophy." *New York Times Magazine,* August 14, 1977, pp. 12ff.
Burke, Edmund. *Works.* 12 vols. Boston: Little, Brown, 1894.
Choptiany, Leonard. "A Critique of John Rawls's Principles of Justice." *Ethics* 83, no. 2 (January, 1973): 146–50.
Clor, Harry M. *Obscenity and Public Morality.* Chicago: University of Chicago Press, 1969.

131

Cohen, Marshall. Review of *A Theory of Justice*. *New York Times Book Review*, July 16, 1972, pp. 1, 16, 18.

Compact Edition of the Oxford English Dictionary. Oxford: Oxford University Press, 1972.

Cox, Richard H. *Locke on War and Peace*. Oxford: Clarendon Press, 1960.

Craig, Leon H. "Contra Contract: A Brief against John Rawls' Theory of Justice." *Canadian Journal of Political Science* 8, no. 1 (March, 1975): 63–81.

―――. "Traditional Political Philosophy and John Rawls' Theory of Justice." *University of Alberta, Department of Political Science, Occasional Papers*, no. 3 (1976).

Cropsey, Joseph. *Political Philosophy and the Issues of Politics*. Chicago: University of Chicago Press, 1977.

―――. *Polity and Economy: An Interpretation of the Principles of Adam Smith*. The Hague: Martinus Nijhoff, 1957.

Daniels, Norman (ed.). *Reading Rawls: Critical Studies of "A Theory of Justice."* New York: Basic Books, n.d.

Decter, Midge. "Looting and Liberal Racism." *Commentary* 64, no. 3 (September, 1977): 48–54.

Diamond, Martin. "Democracy and *The Federalist:* A Reconsideration of the Framers' Intent." *American Political Science Review* 53, no. 1 (March, 1959): 52–68.

―――. "The Dependence of Fact upon 'Value.'" *Interpretation* 2, no. 3 (spring, 1972): 226–35.

―――, Winston M. Fisk, and Herbert Garfinkel. *The Democratic Republic*. 1st ed. Chicago: Rand McNally, 1966.

Eggerman, Richard W. "Moral Theory and Practicality." *Ethics* 84, no. 2 (January, 1974): 174–79.

Frankel, Charles. "The New Egalitarianism and the Old." *Commentary* 56, no. 3 (September, 1973): 54–61.

Friedman, Milton. *Capitalism and Freedom*. Chicago: University of Chicago Press, 1962.

Fullinwider, Robert K. "A Chronological Bibliography of Works on John Rawls' Theory of Justice." *Political Theory*, 5, no. 4 (November, 1977), pp. 561–70.

Goldwin, Robert A. (ed.). *How Democratic Is America?* Chicago: Rand McNally, 1971.

―――. "John Locke." Strauss and Cropsey (eds.), *History of Political Philosophy*, pp. 451–86.

――― (ed.). *Left, Right, and Center*. Chicago: Rand McNally, 1965.

――― (ed.). *On Civil Disobedience*. Chicago: Rand McNally, 1969.

――― (ed.). *100 Years of Emancipation*. Chicago: Rand McNally, 1964.

――― (ed.). *Political Parties, U. S. A*. Chicago: Rand McNally, 1963.

――― (ed.). *Representation and Misrepresentation*. Chicago: Rand McNally, 1968.

Gourevitch, Victor. "Rawls on Justice." *Review of Metaphysics* 28, no. 3 (March, 1975): 485–519.

Hamilton, Alexander, James Madison, and John Jay. *The Federalist*. Ed. Jacob E. Cooke. Middletown, Conn.: Wesleyan University Press, 1961.

Hampshire, Stuart. "A New Philosophy of the Just Society." *New York Review of Books* 18, no. 3 (February 24, 1972): 34–39.

Hare, R. M. "Rawls' Theory of Justice." Daniels (ed.), *Reading Rawls*.

Hart, David K. "Social Equity, Justice, and the Equitable Administrator." *Public Administration Review* 34, no. 1 (January/February, 1974): 3–11.

Hartz, Louis. *The Liberal Tradition in America*. New York: Harcourt, Brace, & World, 1955.

Hassner, Pierre. "Immanuel Kant." Strauss and Cropsey (eds.), *History of Political Philosophy*, pp. 554–93.

Hobbes, Thomas. *Leviathan.* Ed. Michael Oakeshott. Oxford: Basil Blackwell, 1957.
Horwitz, Robert. "Reapportionment in Hawaii." Goldwin (ed.), *Representation and Misrepresentation,* pp. 21–52.
Jaffa, Harry V. "Aristotle." Strauss and Cropsey (eds.), *History of Political Philosophy,* pp. 64–129.
———. "The Nature and Origin of the American Party System." Goldwin (ed.), *Political Parties, U. S. A.,* pp. 59–83.
———. "Reflections on Thoreau and Lincoln: Civil Disobedience and the American Tradition." Goldwin (ed.), *On Civil Disobedience,* pp. 33–60.
———. *Thomism and Aristotelianism.* Chicago: University of Chicago Press, 1952.
Janik, Allan, and Stephen Toulmin. *Wittgenstein's Vienna.* New York: Simon & Schuster, 1973.
Jencks, Christopher, et al. *Inequality.* New York: Basic Books, 1972.
Johnson, Oliver A. "The Kantian Interpretation." *Ethics* 85, no. 1 (October, 1974): 58–66.
Jonas, Hans. *The Phenomenon of Life.* New York: Harper & Row, 1966.
Jouvenel, Bertrand de. *The Ethics of Redistribution.* Cambridge, England: Cambridge University Press, 1951.
Kant, Immanuel. "Perpetual Peace." Lewis White Beck (ed.), *Kant on History.* Indianapolis and New York: Bobbs-Merrill, 1963, pp. 85–135.
———. "Theory and Practice." Carl Friedrich (ed.), *The Philosophy of Kant.* New York: Modern Library, 1949, pp. 412–29.
Koritansky, John C. "Two Forms of the Love of Equality in Tocqueville's Practical Teaching for Democracy." *Polity* 6, no. 4 (summer, 1974): 488–99.
Kristol, Irving. "About Equality." *Commentary* 54, no. 5 (November, 1972): 41–47.
———. "Capitalism, Socialism, and Nihilism." *The Public Interest* 31 (spring, 1973): 3–16.
———. "Republican Virtue vs. Servile Institutions." *The Alternative: An American Spectator* 8, no. 5 (February, 1975): 5–9.
Lincoln, Abraham. *Collected Works.* Ed. Roy P. Basler. 9 vols. New Brunswick, N. J.: Rutgers University Press, 1953.
Lipset, Seymour Martin. "Social Mobility and Equal Opportunity." *The Public Interest* 29 (fall, 1972): 90–108.
Lowenthal, David. "Connecting Church and State Constitutionally." *The Alternative: An American Spectator* 10, no. 8 (May, 1977): 18–20, 30–34.
Lyons, David. "Nature and Soundness of the Contract and Coherence Arguments." Daniels (ed.), *Reading Rawls,* pp. 141–67.
Macpherson, C. B. *Democratic Theory: Essays in Retrieval.* Oxford: Clarendon Press, 1973.
———. *The Political Theory of Possessive Individualism.* Oxford: Clarendon Press, 1962.
Mansfield, Harvey C., Jr. "Hobbes and the Science of Indirect Government." *American Political Science Review* 65, no. 1 (March, 1971): 97–110.
———. "Impartial Representation." Goldwin (ed.), *Representation and Misrepresentation,* pp. 91–114.
———. "Liberal Democracy as a Mixed Regime." *The Alternative: An American Spectator* 8, no. 9 (June/July, 1975): 8–12.
———. "Party Government and the Settlement of 1688." *American Political Science Review* 58, no. 4 (December, 1964): 933–46.
———. "Thomas Jefferson." Morton J. Frisch and Richard A. Stevens (eds.), *American Political Thought.* New York: Scribner's, 1971, pp. 23–50.
McBride, William L. "Social Theory *Sub Specie Aeternitatis:* A New Perspective." *Yale Law Journal* 81, no. 5 (April, 1972): 980–1003.
McCoy, Charles A., and John Playford (eds.). *Apolitical Politics: A Critique of Behavioralism.* New York: Crowell, 1967.

McKeon, Richard (ed.). *The Basic Works of Aristotle.* New York: Random House, 1941.

Mill, John Stuart. *On Liberty, Utilitarianism, and Representative Government.* New York: E. P. Dutton (Everyman's Library), 1951.

Miller, Eugene. "Positivism, Historicism, and Political Inquiry." *American Political Science Review* 66, no. 3 (September, 1972): 796–817.

Montaigne, Michel de. *Essays.* In Donald Frame (transl.), *The Complete Works of Montaigne.* Stanford, Calif.: Stanford University Press, 1957.

Moore, G. E. *Principia Ethica.* 1st ed., Cambridge, England: Cambridge University Press, 1903.

Musgrave, R. A. "Maximin, Uncertainty, and the Leisure Trade-Off." *Quarterly Journal of Economics* 88, no. 4 (November, 1974): 625–32.

Nietzsche, Friedrich. *Beyond Good and Evil.* Transl. Walter Kaufmann. New York: Random House, 1966.

–––. *Thus Spoke Zarathustra. The Portable Nietzsche.* Transl. Walter Kaufmann. New York: Viking, 1954.

Nisbet, Robert. "The Pursuit of Equality." *The Public Interest* 35 (spring, 1974): 103–20.

Nozick, Robert. *Anarchy, State, and Utopia.* New York: Basic Books, 1974.

Orwin, Clifford (University of Toronto). "Compassion as a Source of Democratic Morals." Paper presented at the 1977 meeting of the American Political Science Association.

Plamenatz, John. *Democracy and Illusion: An Examination of Certain Aspects of Modern Democratic Theory.* London and New York: Longman, 1973.

Plattner, Marc F. Review of Peter Singer, *Animal Liberation. Commentary* 61, no. 3 (March, 1976): 76–78.

Rawls, John. "Constitutional Liberty and the Concept of Justice." Carl Friedrich and John Chapman (eds), *Nomos VI: Justice.* New York: Atherton, 1963, pp. 98–125.

–––. "Fairness to Goodness." *Philosophical Review* 84 (October, 1975): 536–54.

–––. "The Independence of Moral Theory." *Proceedings and Addresses of the American Philosophical Association* 48 (1974–75): 5–22.

–––. "Justice as Fairness." *Philosophical Review* 57 (1958): 164–94.

–––. "Outline of a Decision Procedure for Ethics." *Philosophical Review* 50 (1951): 177–97.

–––. "Reply to Alexander and Musgrave." *Quarterly Journal of Economics* 88, no. 4 (November, 1974): 633–55.

–––. Review of Stephen Toulmin, *An Examination of the Place of Reason in Ethics. Philosophical Review* 50 (1951): 572–80.

–––. "The Sense of Justice." *Philosophical Review* 62 (1963): 281–305.

–––. *A Theory of Justice.* Cambridge, Mass.: Belknap Press of Harvard University Press, 1971.

Rosen, Stanley. *Nihilism: A Philosophical Essay.* New Haven, Conn.: Yale University Press, 1969.

Rousseau, Jean-Jacques. *Émile.* Transl. Barbara Foxley. New York: Dutton (Everyman's Library), 1963.

–––. *First and Second Discourses.* Transl. Roger D. Masters and Judith R. Masters. New York: St. Martin's Press, 1964.

–––. *Politics and the Arts.* Transl. Allan Bloom. Glencoe, Ill.: Free Press, 1960.

Schaefer, David L. "Democratic Statesmanship and Morality." *The Alternative: An American Spectator* 8, no. 7 (April, 1975): 15–18.

–––, ed. *The New Egalitarianism: Questions and Challenges.* Port Washington, N.Y.: Kennikat, 1979.

Schlesinger, Steven R. "Civil Disobedience: The Problem of Selective Obedience to Law." *Hastings Constitutional Law Quarterly* 3, no. 4 (fall, 1976): 947–59.

Schrock, Thomas S. "The Liberal Court, the Conservative Court, and Constitutional Jurisprudence." Goldwin (ed.), *Left, Right, and Center,* pp. 87–120.

Shell, Susan Meld. "Kant's Theory of Property." *Political Theory* 6, no. 1 (February, 1978): 75–90.

Singer, Peter. *Animal Liberation.* New York: Random House, 1975.

———. "Philosophers Are Back on the Job." *New York Times Magazine,* July 7, 1974, pp. 6–7, 17–20.

Stevens, Richard G. "The New Republic in More's *Utopia.*" *Political Science Quarterly* 84, no. 3 (September, 1969): 387–411.

Storing, Herbert J. "The Case against Civil Disobedience." Goldwin (ed.), *On Civil Disobedience,* pp. 95–120.

——— (ed. and joint author). *Essays on the Scientific Study of Politics.* New York: Holt, Rinehart, & Winston, 1962.

———. "The School of Slavery: Booker T. Washington." Goldwin (ed.), *100 Years of Emancipation,* pp. 47–79.

Strauss, Leo. "An Epilogue." Storing (ed.), *Essays,* pp. 305–27.

———. *Natural Right and History.* Chicago: University of Chicago Press, 1953.

———. *On Tyranny.* Glencoe, Ill.: Free Press, 1963.

———. *What Is Political Philosophy? and Other Studies.* Glencoe, Ill.: Free Press, 1959.

———, and Joseph Cropsey (eds.). *History of Political Philosophy.* 2d ed. Chicago: Rand McNally, 1972.

Swift, Jonathan. *Gulliver's Travels.* Ed. Louis A. Landa. Cambridge, Mass.: Riverside Press, 1960.

Thurow, Glen E. *Abraham Lincoln and American Political Religion.* Albany, N.Y.: State University of New York Press, 1976.

Tocqueville, Alexis de. *Democracy in America.* Transl. George Lawrence. New York: Harper & Row, 1966.

The Torah. Jewish Publication Society translation. Philadelphia, 1962.

Tucker, Robert C. (ed.). *The Marx-Engels Reader.* New York: Norton, 1972.

Warnock, Mary. *Ethics since 1900.* Oxford: Oxford University Press, 1960.

Washington, Booker T. *Up from Slavery.* 1st ed. New York: Doubleday, Page, 1901.

Washington, George. *Writings of George Washington.* Ed. John C. Fitzpatrick. 39 vols. Washington, D. C.: Superintendent of Documents, 1931–44.

Weiss, Raymond L. "Historicism and Science: Thoughts on Quine." *Dialectica* 29, nos. 2–3 (1975): 157–65.

Weldon, T. D. *The Vocabulary of Politics.* London: Pelican, 1953.

Wills, Garry, "Ethical Problems." *New York Times Book Review,* June 25, 1978, p. 13.

Winthrop, Delba (University of Virginia). "Aristotle and Theories of Justice." Paper presented at the 1976 meeting of the American Political Science Association.

Wittgenstein, Ludwig. *Philosophical Investigations.* 2d ed. Oxford: Basil Blackwell, 1963.

Wolfe, Tom. *Radical Chic & Mau-Mauing the Flak Catchers.* New York: Farrar, Straus & Giroux, 1970.

Wolff, Robert Paul. *Understanding Rawls.* Princeton, N. J.: Princeton University Press, 1977.

Zuckert, Michael P. (Carleton College), "Justice Deserted: A Critique of John Rawls's *A Theory of Justice.*" Unpublished paper.

———. "Justice Deserted, or What Is Really Wrong with Rawls." Unpublished paper.

INDEX

Intuitionism, 11, 22-23, 91-92, 101-02

Jaffa, Harry V., 117, 122, 124, 127
Janik, Allan, 128, 129
Jefferson, Thomas, 82, 127, 130
Jencks, Christopher, 123
Johnson, Oliver A., 125, 127
Jonas, Hans, 116
Jouvenel, Bertrand de, 123

Kant, Immanuel, 9, 24, 30, 39, 53-54, 74-75, 82, 99, 120, 122, 124, 125
King, Martin Luther, Jr., 125
Koritansky, John C., 126
Kripke, Saul, 117
Kristol, Irving, 81-82, 108-09, 121, 129

Liberty, 31-33, 41, 43, 45-53, 60, 71-72, 88-90, 119
Lincoln, Abraham, 82, 123
Lipset, Seymour Martin, 123
Locke, John, xi, 9, 24, 30, 38, 39, 41, 50, 58, 103-04, 114, 121, 125, 129
Lowenthal, David, 121
Loyola, St. Ignatius, 60, 119
Lyons, David, 120

Machiavelli, Niccolò, 101
Macpherson, C. B., 120, 126
Madison, James, 82
Mansfield, Harvey C., Jr., 120, 121, 122, 125, 129, 130
Marx, Karl, xi, 47, 76, 78, 125
Maximin rule, 33-34
McBride, William L., 126
McCoy, Charles A., 126
Mill, John Stuart, 88-90, 119
Miller, Eugene, 128, 129
Montaigne, Michel de, 99, 103-04, 121, 124, 127, 129
More, St. Thomas, 122
Musgrave, R. A., 126, 130

New Left, 59
Nietzsche, Friedrich, xi, 22, 76, 102-03, 117, 125, 126, 128
Nisbet, Robert, 117, 126
Nozick, Robert, 5

Orwin, Clifford, 129

"Perfectionism," 11, 22, 89, 126
Plamenatz, John, 126
Plato, x, 9, 10, 13, 72, 76, 93, 99, 100, 117, 118, 119, 124, 126, 127, 129
Plattner, Marc F., 123
Playford, John, 126

Polemarchus, 127
"Primary" goods, 31, 37, 49-50, 75, 79-80, 113-14, 120

Quine, W. V., 128

Religion, 27, 37-38, 48-51, 74, 113-14, 121-22
Rosen, Stanley, 127, 128
Rousseau, Jean-Jacques, xi, 9, 15, 24, 30, 38, 39, 50, 51, 73-74, 117, 120, 121, 123

Schlesinger, Steven R., 124
Schrock, Thomas S., 121
Self-respect, self-esteem, 51, 67, 72-74, 77-79, 81-82, 124
Shell, Susan Meld, 122
Sidgwick, Henry, 21
Singer, Peter, 123, 127
Smith, Adam, 50, 121
Socrates, x, 9, 18, 69, 71, 76, 92-94, 99
Social union, idea of, 69-70
Stevens, Richard G., 122
Storing, Herbert J., xii, 119, 124, 125, 126
Strauss, Leo, xii, 10, 120, 126, 127, 128, 129
Swift, Jonathan, 122

Thrasymachus, 82, 93
Thurow, Glen E., 121
Tocqueville, Alexis de, 3, 58-59, 82, 108, 115, 126
Toulmin, Stephen, 124, 128, 129
Tucker, Robert C., 125

Utilitarianism, 11, 20-22, 86-87, 89, 101-02, 120, 127-28

"Veil of ignorance," 28-30, 37-38, 43-45, 110-11

Warnock, Mary, 128, 129
Washington, Booker T., 77
Washington, George, 121
Weiss, Raymond L., 128
Weldon, T. D., 128
Wills, Garry, 117
Wittgenstein, Ludwig, xii, 102, 128
Wolfe, Tom, 129
Wolff, Robert Paul, 118, 120, 126

X, Malcolm, 125
Xenophon, 93

Zarathustra, 76
Zuckert, Michael P., 5, 122, 123